First and Thirty

Social Upheaval in the 1970s' South and the High School Football Game That Broke an Epic Losing Streak

Buck Buchanan

First and Thirty

Social Upheaval in the 1970s' South and the High School Football Game That Broke an Epic Losing Streak

Published by
  Broadway Ventures, LLC
  260 Manning Road SW, Unit 130
  Marietta, GA 30064

Copyright ©2015, Buck Buchanan

Cover Illustration: Cindy Frazier

ISBN: 978-0-692-49275-8

$16.99us

This book is dedicated:

To the memory of Chattanooga High, a school that for over 100 years was one of the top public schools in the state. Unfortunately, today, the once-proud school is just a memory, but those who walked the halls of the City High on 3rd Street, and the newer version on Dallas Road, will not forget what made the school great: the teachers and administrators who created a culture for learning, along with a sense of school pride; its rich traditions; and the many alumni who went on to successful lives and careers.

To the 1970 Dynamo football team and coaches, who came from different backgrounds, but once on the field, came together as one. This was a group that dealt with challenges from the off season to the last game played.

To my wife, who put up with me during those high school years.

Acknowlegments

To Marc Williams for being supportive of my first writing venture by helping me connect with old friends during the researching process.

To former teammates Pat Petty, Eddie Roberson, Bill Wilder, Lee Abelson, Tommy Richmond, David Soloff, Mike O'Neil, and Marvin Day, who shared their memories of those days with me.

To Arch Trimble and Denny Cornett, who passed away before the book was completed, but shared their stories before their fatal illnesses took their lives.

To Sammye and Kenny Smith, who shared their memories with me.

To my wife Cindy, who helped me gather the pictures for the book, supplied her original artwork for the cover, and whom I constantly asked if she remembered events, people, etc. Her recollections were sometimes slightly different than mine, but in the end, I had the literary license, so I put my version in print. I hope when she reads it, she'll agree.

To Deke Castleman, who edited my book and guided me through the publishing process. I found him to be my critic, my cheerleader, my coach, and my advisor. He taught me more about writing than any of my English teachers did, while making the process fun. Of course, this time, I was paying attention.

Contents

Prologue

The vista from Rock City, a popular tourist attraction at the top of Lookout Mountain in Chattanooga, Tennessee, is stunning. The Tennessee River winds through the mountainous terrain below and it's said you can see seven states from its viewing points. But the mountain looks out on more than space; it also watches time roll along, and as the clock struck midnight on January 1, 1970, both a new year and a new decade were ushered in. The sixties were over. What would the next 10 years bring? The high-school kids in Hamilton County, Tennessee, would experience the changes, both personal and social, firsthand as they transitioned from teenagers to adults.

The sixties brought on more social changes in our country than any decade since the Roaring Twenties. In human terms, they started as a clean-cut conservative fifties' lad and ended up as a long-haired free-spirited flower child. The word "pot" no longer described a vessel to cook in; it now had a whole new meaning, as drugs shifted from the back alleys to the college campuses. Similarly, people of color moved from the back of the bus to the front page of the newspaper. The worldwide battle between democracy and communism led to the brink of Armageddon over a nuclear showdown with the Soviet Union during the Cuban Missile Crisis. National leaders were shot down in public, while Vietnam War protests challenged the foundation of the union.

Technology exploded, perfectly symbolized by a man stepping down from a spacecraft onto the surface on the moon as the world watched, live and in color. The computer age arrived, with large mainframe computers now used by government, universities, and industry. Electric typewriters were slowly replacing manual typewriters in the workplace.

It was a time when fast sporty cars were the trend as automobile companies tried to find ways to get more horsepower out of V-8 engines. They were gas guzzlers, but a gallon of gas cost less than 35 cents. Most cars just off the showroom floor could easily do 120 mph and some could hit 150. The speed limit on the freeways was 75, which meant that cruising at 90 was the standard pace. And though most cars now came with lap seat belts in front, they were seldom used.

Of course, life went on. Kids grew up and dealt with the changes as best they could, but kids in the South probably faced more challenges than those in other parts of the country, because they had lived with segregation for generations. A change to equal rights for black people would take some time. But even as society changes, most traditions carry on and one of the most prevalent, especially in the South, was a love of sports.

In the summer, baseball teams competed in every town and city throughout the South, from Little League to minor league, from semi pro to America Legion. Southern folks love their baseball. In 1966, the Milwaukee Braves moved to Atlanta and quickly became the team of the South. It was the first major-league team of any sport south of the Mason Dixon line and Southerners took great pride in having their own professional team.

When summer gave way, fall football took center stage.

On Saturdays, college campuses big or small were converted from centers of higher learning to football meccas for students, alumni, and fans. The history of Southern college-football games dated back to the 19th century. The University of Georgia and Auburn University had been playing against each other almost every year since 1892. And as Saturdays were reserved for college games, Friday was the night for high-school football. The passion at these games was every bit as intense as at the colleges.

A few months earlier, in the fall of 1969, I was sitting in the stands, watching the final seconds count down. The final score would be 29 to 6. Chattanooga High School had once again lost to Central High School and its legendary coach, E. B. "Red" Etter. It had now been 30 years since "City," which was what everyone called Chattanooga High, had defeated Central. Oh well, maybe next year the City Dynamos could end the streak and beat the Central Pounders.

I was a junior in high school and had been attending City for only about three weeks. I would have much preferred to be on the field playing, rather than in the stands spectating, but I wasn't eligible to be on the team this season. I couldn't help but think that if I'd been playing, maybe City could have won. I'd have to wait until next year to get a chance to play against the hated rival from across town.

Fast-forward to a year later, the fall of 1970, when the Chattanooga High Dynamo football team was picked by local sports writers to be one of the best, if not the best, in the city. Some knowledgeable observers thought this would be the best team the school had ever fielded. It was Bob Davis's third year as the head football coach. In the past two years, he'd given a school better known for its baseball and basketball teams a respectable football program. But on the field itself, one major obstacle lay in the way of the surging Dynamos. Would 1970, when the players were dealing with life as teenagers during the controversies of war, desegregation, drugs, and a profoundly changing society, be the year that tide would turn and City would finally beat Central?

Chapter 1

A Tennessee Town

I, Carlton Blaine Buchanan, was born in Chattanooga in December 1952. My father, E. Blaine Buchanan, was a lawyer who had grown up on a farm in Cleveland, Tennessee. During the Depression, he worked as a bookkeeper while taking night classes at the Chattanooga College of Law. He graduated, passed the Bar exam, and began practicing law in 1940. He mainly worked as a one-man civil lawyer, where he specialized in interstate commerce, but also worked with small businesses in the area.

My mother, Irene Cox, was also raised on a family farm in the central Tennessee town of Murfreesboro. In the late 1930s, she moved with her family to Red Bank, Tennessee, as her father took a job with the newly formed TVA.

E. Blaine and Irene met while they were working in Chattanooga and were married in 1935.

Chattanooga is a typical Southern town located in the southeastern corner of Tennessee on the Georgia line. It's on the Tennessee River and sits between two mountains and a large ridge. Lookout Mountain rises from the west side of the river, across from Signal Mountain on the east side. These mountains form the northern boundary of the city. The south side of the city is protected by Missionary Ridge.

The area was first inhabited by the Creek Indians. Its location on the river made it an ideal spot as a trading outpost. The name Chattanooga supposedly comes from an Indian name that meant "Rock Coming to a Point," which was believed to describe the shape of Lookout Mountain.

The waterway and later the railroads provided the commercial foundation of the city and turned Chattanooga into a key transportation hub in the South. The area became a strategic point near the end of the Civil War; whichever side controlled Chattanooga would control the gateway to Dixie. During the Civil War, three major battles were fought in and around the city. The South won the battle of Chickamauga, which was fought south of the city in Georgia in September 1863. The defeated Union Army retreated to Chattanooga to regroup. In November, the Southern forces attempted to retake the town, but lost the battles of Lookout Mountain and Missionary Ridge. These two victories ultimately led to Sherman's capture of Atlanta and his famed "March to the Sea," which split the South in two and eventually led to the defeat of the Confederacy.

After the Civil War, like most Southern cities, Chattanooga had to rebuild. Fortunately, much of its economic base remained intact and helped expedite its recovery. For the most part, the railroad survived the war and transported much of the goods needed for the rebuilding of the South.

The city's reputation as a transportation hub was elevated in 1941 with the hit song, "Chattanooga Choo Choo," made famous by Glenn Miller and His Orchestra. The song gained national popularity and turned the city into a familiar name. The railroads and the river continued to be the source of economic development. The steel industry, banking, insurance, and even ties to the Atlanta-based Coca-Cola dynasty also drove the development of the city. Certainly, the establishment of the TVA (Tennessee Valley Authority) during the thirties also helped contribute to growth. In 1969, Chattanooga was the fourth largest city in the state of Tennessee, as well as the seat for Hamilton County.

Like most other Southern cities, Chattanooga was segregated at the turn of the new decade. The majority of blacks in Hamilton County lived in Chattanooga between 3rd and 9th streets, with other black sections scattered around the county. The affluent whites lived on Lookout Mountain, Missionary Ridge, and portions of Signal Mountain, and in the Riverview community near the Chattanooga Country Club in North Chattanooga.

When it came to education, schools were broken down into city and county public schools and private schools. In 1969, there were five city public high schools: Chattanooga or City, Brainerd, Kirkman, Howard, and Riverside. Howard and Riverside were all-black schools and Kirkman was the trade school. In the county, the bigger towns had their own schools, such as East Ridge, Red Bank, Soddy, and Daisy. Then there was the catch-all and largest high school in the county, Chattanooga Central. Notre Dame was the only Catholic school in the community. Girls Preparatory School (GPS) was the all-white all-girls private school; the all-boys military-style schools were Baylor and McCallie.

Schools in the South had slowly begun to integrate. This began in 1954 after the Supreme Court ruling of Brown v. Brown, the landmark United States Supreme Court case, in which the Court declared that state laws establishing separate public schools for black and white students were unconstitutional. In Chattanooga, the integration process began in the mid-sixties. The first step was to allow anyone within the city or county school districts to attend any school they wanted, regardless of where they lived. Prior to this, blacks could only attend the all-black schools. This "soft" integration plan seemed to work, though a couple hundred years of segregation history still had to be undone.

Chapter 2

A New School

My sister Betty Gayle was born in 1942. She was married and living in Knoxville by the time I got to high school. The Buchanans—my father and mother and I—lived in the white-collar Shepherd Hills neighborhood of about 150 homes located in the Brainerd area of Chattanooga. Our one-level red-brick ranch-style house sat on a lot backed up to Pleasant Garden, a cemetery that had been deeded by Benjamin Franklin for the burial of slaves. The grounds weren't well-kept and most of the graves were covered with uncut grass and weeds. Trees and bushes grew randomly, headstones had fallen over, and some graves were sunk below the ground line. Still, it was an active cemetery. As kids, we played war games on the grounds and in the surrounding woods. On the days of a funeral, we climbed up on the roof of my dad's workshop on the back edge of the property and had a great view of the graveside service. The funerals were always impressive, everyone dressed in their Sunday best and always lots of loud singing, preaching, and crying. The celebration of life and death was quite a spectacle and sometimes lasted for a couple of hours. It was far different from the short somber white funerals I'd attended.

I'd spent eighth, ninth, and tenth grades at Castle Heights Military Academy in Lebanon, Tennessee. Scholastics were not my focus, as I was much more interested in sports and having fun. My sister Betty had gone on to GPS and done well. She then went on to graduate from the University of Tennessee. As far as academics went, she'd set the bar fairly high, so my dad expected the same from me. He wanted me to go to a private school and McCallie was the logical choice, since it was only two miles from our house. The only problem was my grades weren't good enough for me to get in. So after elementary school, I attended Dalewood Junior High in the Brainerd district. This was the first time I'd gone to school with black kids. Frankly, it was no big deal to me. I'd grown up around them and they were just regular folk.

In seventh grade, I had a C-plus average and my parents were afraid I wouldn't graduate from high school, ending up as a ditch digger or something. Castle Heights, a military boarding school with structure and discipline, seemed to be the answer. At the time, I figured it would be okay, because of their sports programs. I also loved John Wayne's war movies and thought the military was cool. After all, if John Wayne could be a soldier, surely I could be a military cadet.

So at the beginning of eighth grade, it was off to an all-boys, all-white, military academy. Upon arrival, I received a couple sets of uniforms, everyday and dress. The uniforms resembled West Point's gray style. Anytime we were out of the barracks, we had to be in uniform. Then there was the marching. Every day, we marched to breakfast, lunch, and dinner. Then we marched in the afternoons. Hell, if the varsity had a football game, we marched to the game. We woke up early in the morning to the sound of "Revelry" and went to bed to the sound of "Taps."

After two months at Castle Heights, I concluded that I belonged anywhere but a school with so much military and structure. Nonetheless, it took two and half more years to convince my parents of it. Finally, after my sophomore year, it was goodbye military school and hello public school. I could barely imagine what it would be like to go to school with girls and not have to march anywhere.

In fall 1969, it looked like I'd be a junior at Chattanooga High School. But there was talk about me going to Central High. My dad and the Central coach, Red Etter, were friends. Before I was born my dad, mom, and sister had lived down the street from the Etters. E. Blaine really admired Coach Etter and wanted me to play for him. The problem was that Central had just moved to a new location almost 20 miles east of where it had been. If the school had remained at the old location, which was just two miles away, I most likely would have been a Purple Pounder.

Luckily, I wanted to go to City High. It had a great reputation and was considered the best non-private school in the area. Another contributing factor was that my cousins Mary Lynn and Connie Bates had gone there. Their dad, Conrad Bates, was a chemistry teacher there and had been for over 30 years. As a kid growing up, I'd always heard about City High and how cool it was. E. Blaine also thought it was a good school for me, maybe because he was thinking that Uncle Conrad could keep an eye on me. So the home of the Dynamos seemed to be the obvious place to go.

Located in North Chattanooga on Dallas Road, the school was deep in tradition. Chattanooga High's first class graduated in 1879, making it the oldest secondary school in the South. Throughout its history, the high school had occupied various locations in the city; in summer 1963, it moved to the old W. Welland Estate, or the "Hill" as some people called it. It sat like a beacon on that hill, with its two-level concrete, stone, and glass façade.

Out in front of the school stood the maroon dynamo, which accounted for the school symbol and nickname. I always assumed the name was taken from the Chickamauga (hydroelectric) Dam, which used dynamos to generate electricity. Compared to other schools, whose teams were named Lions, Tigers, and Bears, ours was certainly unique. We didn't have to worry about anyone else copying it. I'm fairly sure we were the only Dynamos in the South, and maybe the whole country, for that matter.

City High had about 1,500 students in three grades. Most lived in North Chattanooga, but there were plenty others from all over the Chattanooga area. The school was made up of rich, poor, blacks, whites, rednecks, preppies, and hippies. Though there were only 100 or so black kids, the student body was probably the most diversified in the city. It was also a landing place for those kids who, like me, left one of the local private schools for one reason or another.

I entered 11th grade in September 1969, with the sixties ending and serious changes in the air, for me and the world.

Chapter 3

What a Year Already

When the school year started in September, 1969 had already been a memorable year. On a national level, in January, Richard Nixon had been sworn in as the 37th president of the United States. The Vietnam War continued to be a daily news topic and some of the most memorable events in the country's history happened during the summer.

In July, Mary Jo Kopechne was riding in a car driven by U.S. Senator Ted Kennedy when Kennedy drove off a bridge and into a tidal creek on Chappaquiddick Island. The senator was able to swim free and left the scene of the accident, while Kopechne drowned. It wasn't until the next day before Kopechne's body and the car were finally recovered. Kennedy received a two-month suspended jail sentence for leaving the scene of an accident. The scandal put an end to any chance he might have had to follow in his brother's footsteps to the White House.

A few days later, Apollo11 became the first manned spacecraft to land on the moon. It was also the first time a man actually walked on the moon's surface.

A few weeks later, a string of murders were committed in California under the direction of a convicted felon and musician, Charles Manson.

In mid-August, a music festival that was billed as "Three Days of Peace & Music" was held at Max Yasgur's 600-acre farm in upstate New York, 43 miles southwest of the town of Woodstock. During the sometimes rainy weekend, 32 musical acts performed outdoors before an audience of approximately 400,000 young people.

Back in Chattanooga, I was getting ready for my new school. I welcomed the change from a military environment to a public school. My real challenge was in being a new kid. Entering high school as a junior was tough, because the groups and the cliques had formed the year before. Although I'd lived in Chattanooga all my life, I'd spent the past three years going to school out of town. In addition, most of the kids I'd gone to elementary school with were attending Brainerd High or one of the private schools. Being new wouldn't be easy, but it still beat Castle Heights.

Of course, one of the quickest ways to get accepted in a new school is to get involved. My ticket in was football. The previous year at Castle Heights, I'd played on the varsity team, even though I was a sophomore. Not only was I fast, but I wasn't afraid to hit anyone, despite weighing only 135 pounds. So I earned a spot on the suicide squads or the kickoff and punt teams. I got to play in all the games and was one of only three underclassmen to letter on the 1968 team.

Earlier in the summer before school started, I met with City's Head Football Coach, Bob Davis. Davis looked like a football coach. He was a former quarterback and stood about 5'10", was bald, and had a small beer belly and a Bob Hope sloped nose. For a Southerner, he was a fast-talking guy. My Uncle Conrad had told Coach Davis I was coming to school. So before my meeting, Davis talked to the coach at Castle Heights. He knew about my football resumé and was excited to have me on the team.

There was only one catch and Coach Davis was quick to get to the point. "I'm sorry, son, but it turns out you're ineligible to play on this year's varsity team."

My jaw dropped. I was stunned.

He explained the state rules for transferring students. "In Tennessee high school sports, the only way you can transfer schools and play the next season is if your family physically moves its residence from one school district to another."

"Well, Coach, technically I lived in Lebanon, Tennessee, last year and was moving back home," I countered.

"I'm aware of that and I argued the same point to the Tennessee High School Athletic Association. But rules are rules and your family would have had to move for you to be eligible to play this year. Now, you can practice with the team and play junior varsity during the season, but not varsity."

To myself, I said, "Screw it." It crushed my ego to be relegated to playing JV my junior year. I told Coach Davis, "Thanks, but no thanks."

Which is why I was sitting in the stands, watching Central whip City for the 29th time in a row. Worst of all, it wasn't just football I was banned from; I couldn't play any school sports my junior year.

So much for fitting in by getting involved.

Chapter 4

School Starts

Just as City High had done six years earlier by moving from its long-time location on 3rd Street to its new location in North Chattanooga, Central High was moving its campus. After being at the same location for as long as most people could remember (60 years), the county's largest school would now be located 20 miles from the Dodds Avenue campus. The school had to move, because the old building was inadequate to house the rapidly expanding progressive high school.

Up until the move, City and Central had been less than 10 miles apart. This close distance was partly responsible for the rivalry between the two schools. Central was also one of Chattanooga's first public high schools, so the two had been competing against each other since the early 1900s. Central was highly acclaimed for both its scholastic and athletic accomplishments.

Central's school colors were purple and gold, so its teams originally went by the name Purple Warriors. But during the thirties, they had so dominated that a local sportswriter began to describe them by the way they often "pounded" their opponents, and the "Purple Pounders" became their nickname. The name was symbolized by a logo of a purple hammer hitting an anvil.

School started the day after Labor Day. I had to go to orientation the Thursday before the holiday. It was mandatory for new students, who met in the school auditorium where the principal, Dr. Jim Henry, along with a couple of teachers reviewed the upcoming year and what to expect. Most of the students in attendance were sophomores, but there were a few juniors like me. After the meeting, we broke up into small groups that were led by seniors to tour the campus and get the lay of the land. My group assembled by bronze statues of Abraham Lincoln and Robert E. Lee. I thought these statues were odd, given that neither man ever stepped foot in this part of Tennessee.

As I approached City on the following Tuesday, I thought that it was tough enough being the new kid at school, but it was even tougher with a name like Carlton. I often wondered how in the hell I wound up with such a name. What was wrong with Matthew, Mark, or John? My sister told me I'd been named after a hotel and I didn't think it was the Ritz. I didn't want to ask any more questions after that explanation. I would just be Carlton or whatever anyone wanted to call me.

Since I couldn't play football, my strategy to get accepted in the new school was blown out of the water. What now? Well, first I planned to start reconnecting with the kids I knew. Admittedly, it wasn't much of a plan, with only 15 or 20 kids on the list. And I quickly found even that to be difficult, because most of these kids were already in their cliques. At 15 and 16 years old, it wasn't cool to act like you knew a new guy, much less bring him into your circle of friends. So after acknowledging me briefly, most of my old acquaintances acted like I had the plague.

It was about a 15-mile drive to City High from Shepard Hills. I carpooled to school with two seniors who lived in our neighborhood, Chris Boehm and Martha Killeffer. I'd known both for a long time. Martha lived across the street from me. They introduced me to a few people, but these became casual acquaintances.

The gym was located on the upper level on the east side and the auditorium was located on the west side of the building. The Commons and the classrooms made up the core of the structure. The Commons was the central point of the school. As you entered the school from the front, you walked up the steps from the parking lot and entered the Commons, which served as the lunch room, the gathering spot, the dance room, and the crossroad between classes.

The school office was located to the right of the Commons just as you entered the main entrance. This was also where the principal's offices were located. Dr. Jim Henry was the principal and Coach Jim Phifer was the assistant principal, in charge of discipline. Dr. Henry was raised in Chattanooga and graduated from City in 1941, where he was an All-City football player for the Dynamos. He later returned to teach and coach at the school. Coach Phifer was also from Chattanooga where he attended Notre Dame and played football. So football was important to them, but discipline and running a top-notch school were their main priorities.

The official school clock was located on the back wall on the right side of the Commons, at the center of the campus. It was under this clock that the "guys" sat every morning before school. Between four and eight boys hung out there, wearing blue jeans with baseball undershirts and Converse "Chuck Taylor" sneakers.

A few days into the school year, I noticed a familiar face in the group under the clock, Kenny Smith. Kenny was from East Lake and we played baseball against each during elementary school. One year we developed a friendship at a summer camp we both attended.

I later learned that Kenny had followed an interesting road to City High. The closest high school to East Lake was Central on Dodds Avenue. He'd grown up as a Central fan. The summer after ninth grade, he played baseball with Central's Optimists team and he planned to continue his athletic career as a Purple Pounder. On the first day of school, however, he learned that the baseball coach wanted his players to concentrate on baseball and not play any other sport. This was disheartening for Kenny; he really wanted to play basketball as well as baseball. So he considered his options. Kenny had met the City High basketball coach and assistant principal, Jim Phifer, at a summer camp. Coach Phifer had left a positive impression, so Kenny went to the pay phone in the school lobby, fished out a dime, and placed a call to City High.

Surprisingly, the coach came on the phone. Kenny asked, "Coach, can I play basketball and baseball at City?"

Phifer said, "Every kid in school can come out for any team, so come on." He then instructed Kenny to come to City, get enrolled, and attend an "unofficial" basketball practice at the school that afternoon. He even picked up the carless Smith near Central and drove him to City. Central lost a good athlete that day.

Coach Phifer drove him home after practice. Now Kenny had to tell his parents that he'd changed schools, not only without their permission but their knowledge!

The next day, I noticed that Kenny was sitting under the clock before school. I went up and asked him how things were going. When he acted like he didn't know me, I turned and walked away. Oh well, I thought, just part of being the new guy. I knew our paths would cross again and things would be different. Meanwhile, I'd keep looking for old friends to connect with.

Chapter 5

Out for the Year

School started at 8:20 a.m. with homeroom, where the teacher called roll and student council representatives read the daily announcements. After homeroom came first, second, and third periods; fourth period was followed by lunch, or lunch followed by fourth period. Next we had activity, fifth, and sixth periods. Sixth period was really for the after-school programs, such as sports, band, drill team, cheerleading, etc.

Activity period was the time for school meetings in the auditorium. It could be a full-school assembly, a pep rally, a performance, an inspirational talk, and so forth. You were required to sit with your homeroom and the teachers took roll; being absent from activity period earned one detention.

Chattanooga High offered a wide range of classes: English, math, science, and history; Spanish, French, Russian, and Latin (we didn't hear much Russian or Latin spoken in the halls); algebra, geometry, and trigonometry; physics, biology, chemistry, and even aerospace; economics, Bible, psychology, and sociology; and business education, home ec, shop, and mechanical drawing. They were taught by a great core of teachers, some of whom had spent their entire careers at City. Over the years, the school had produced a number of very prominent and successful alumni.

The school offered a variety of social clubs. The girls had clubs like Optimist, Lioness Boosters, Anchors, Tri-Hi-Y, and La Sertomiss. The more popular boys clubs were Leo, Key, Civitans, Hi-Y, and Junior Optimist. There was even the Peoples Club for the free spirits or hippies of the school.

With school underway, I had to start getting into the flow and developing a network of friends. I knew I had to do it by making one friend at a time. It would take time, but I was determined to be included in the school's social circles by Christmas. I started getting to know the kids in my homeroom. Also, I'd been in the Key Club at Castle Heights, which was considered the cool club there. So it made sense for me to get involved with the Key Club at City High, where surely it would be just as cool.

Ricky Brown sat next to me in homeroom. He was friendly and he gave me daily advice concerning what to expect at City. He was also a member of the Key Club. At the first meeting, I found another old friend from elementary school, Lee Abelson. Lee was a member of the football team; he'd also been the new kid in his sophomore year, so he understood what I was going through. Ricky also introduced me to one of his good friends in the Key Club, Eddie Francisco. So between Eddie, Ricky, and Lee, it appeared that the Key Club might be a good place for me. The Key Club's claim to fame was they produced a school directory.

Lee's leg was in a cast and he told me the story of what happened. Although he was a big kid, he hadn't planned on playing football. So he got involved making signs for the football games backstage—where Miss Pryor held court.

Miss Katherine Pryor was a short round white-haired old spinster who epitomized City High. She ran the drama and stage programs, the Student Council, and pretty much anything else she wanted to be involved with. She was in full control of her programs and was very picky as to who could participate, but if you were part of her inner circle, you had it made. Like a mother hen, she looked after her students, who were referred to as the "Brownies" (because they brown-nosed Queen Katherine).

Miss Pryor was anti-sports and didn't care too much for

jocks. It was believed that the only reason her stage kids made banners for football games was so she could control the content. She also didn't like the Civitans, and if one of her Brownies went out on a date with a Civitan, she could be expelled from the Pryor circle. She was the self-appointed morality police at the school. At dances, she patrolled the dance floor, separating couples who she felt were getting too close. Heaven forbid if she smelled alcohol on your breath at a school function.

Katherine Pryor had been at CHS so long that she'd taught Lee's mother when she was a student there. So Lee had a connection to getting back stage and making signs, which was a fairly prestigious job in Dynamo society. Through his sophomore year, the football coaches were after him to try out for the team and he finally signed up to play, in part to get out from under Miss Pryor's control.

Lee made it through spring practice and the summer two-a-day practices until one day, near the end of summer, Lee was trying to make a block when it seemed like half the team fell on his extended right leg, bending in a direction it was not supposed to go.

The next day, Lee came to practice, but he was in serious pain and his knee was so swollen that he couldn't bend it. Coach Davis sent him to see the doctor at Campbell Clinic just east of downtown Chattanooga and Lee got into his car, a straight-shift Chevrolet Malibu.

Dr. Dodds, the team doctor, found that Abelson had torn ligaments and needed surgery, which was done the next day, culminating in a full leg cast. When he checked out of the hospital, Lee was handed a pair of crutches and sent home. As he hobbled to the parking lot, it dawned on him: How in the world could he operate a car that requires two good legs, one for the clutch and one for the accelerator?

But first, he had to figure out how to get into the driver's seat with one good leg and one leg that was immobilized completely straight. He got his right leg splayed out across the bench seat and the left leg on the clutch. Next he realized that pressing the accelerator with a right leg completely straight in a cast was just not going to happen. Then he conceived of using the crutch to push the pedal. But how was he going to hold the crutch and the steering wheel at the same time? Then it occurred to him that he could push the seat up and jam the crutch against the seat to force the pedal down. Finally, he let out the clutch with his good leg and off he went. Somehow, using his good left leg and a crutch, he managed to get home in one piece.

So Lee'd had an interesting journey over the past 12 months, going from sign maker to football player and having to sit out the year. Sitting on the sidelines was something else we both had in common.

After attending a couple Key Club meetings, I knew that it really wasn't my style. Although it might have been a good way to meet girls, I didn't want to go around school and collect addresses and phone numbers for the school directory. Other than Ricky Brown and Lee, I didn't have a lot in common with the rest of the club members. They weren't really into sports and they seemed more focused on school work than hell-raising. I much preferred raising hell to studying.

So again, I adjusted my plan for inserting myself into the school's social circles.

Chapter 6

A Tour of Shoney's

I had Miss Moore for English. The youngest teacher in the department, she was in her thirties and she had a good sense of humor. Her classroom was fairly large and was across from the gym. It only took a couple days with Miss Moore before it was clear to me that this wasn't the English class for the Rhodes scholars. It seemed like Miss Moore had to explain the daily assignment to several students two or three times before they got it. Some of the assignments were as simple as writing a two-page essay about what we did the previous summer. At first, I thought they were just trying to give her a hard time, but as the days went on, I realized they truly didn't understand much.

Then there was a guy who sat on the other side of the room and made weird sounds. All of a sudden, an odd noise would ring out—a chirping bird, a random word, or a soft whistle. It took me a couple of classes before I figured out that the culprit was Randy C. Gray, a linebacker on the football team.

Randy C. also did strange voice inflections when reading poetry. One day we were taking turns reading poetry and he was asked to read "Stopping by Woods on a Snowy Evening" by Robert Frost. He read the first verse in a normal tone; then he got to the second verse.

My little horse must think it queer
To stop without a farmhouse near
Between the woods and frozen lake
The darkest evening of the year.

When he got to the word "queer," he pronounced it in a high shrill voice. He paused, then continued in his normal tone until he using his high shrill voice to emphasize the word "year." Miss Moore tried to keep a straight face, while the rest of the class broke out in laughter. That was when I knew why the youngest teacher got this particular class: The other English teachers had way too much seniority to deal with this bunch of cut-ups.

As school went on, I met a few more kids. One day in the hall, I ran into another familiar face, Rick Spencer. Rick and I had gone to Dalewood together and been good friends in those days. Rick was a clean-cut guy who didn't smoke or drink, but could cuss like a sailor. He was an only child whose father had died when he was a young boy. He and his mom, who worked for a church, lived in a modest house in the Brainerd area. Rick was a talented musician and played the organ in a band from time to time. He really liked fast cars, but drove his mom's old Dodge Dart. He worked part-time at the drug store in Dalewood. Since we lived near each other, it didn't take too long before Rick and I began to occasionally hang out together.

As far as Rick was concerned, Shoney's on Brainerd Road was where the action was. A popular hangout for teenagers, you could meet your friends, find a date, set up a drag race, or pick a fight there. It was busy during the week, but on Friday and Saturday nights, the place was packed. Shoney's was "Home of the Big Boy." Though mainly a burger joint, it offered other dishes for breakfast, lunch, and dinner. You could eat inside or sit in your car and get service. Curbside, you parked in one of two covered parking areas. Two parking stalls faced each other, so the cars were parked hood to hood; 24 cars fit under each canopy. You ordered from an intercom box at the driver's window and a carhop brought out your food and collected the money.

Shoney's was the place for cruising, the big nighttime sport for teenagers. It was kind of like the Indians circling the wagons, but at Shoney's, it meant circling the parking lot. It was also the place to show off your car—if you had a car to show off. Rick's Dodge Dart wasn't one of these. If your car was fast enough, you could arrange drag races for later that night on I-75 just past the Concord Road exit. The winner earned Shoney's bragging rights.

The Brainerd Shoney's was mainly Brainerd and Central High's turf, though occasionally Tyner High kids ventured over. The local hoods also hung out there. Sometimes fights broke out, but this was fairly rare; a policeman was usually stationed there during the peak cruising hours.

Rick wanted me to go with him to Shoney's to pick up girls. One night I agreed to go with him. A couple miles before we got there, Rick pulled over at a Kayo filling station. Noticing he had a full tank, I asked him why he was stopping.

He said, "I need to get some rubbers, in case I get lucky."

I said to myself, "I hope they have a good shelf life." I did appreciate Rick's optimism, but I also knew we were no different than other 16- or 17-year-old boys. I bet if you checked all the boys' wallets at City High, half of them had a pack of rubbers in them. It must have come from their Boy Scout days of being prepared. Oh well, it wasn't a big investment; after all, for only a quarter, you could get a three-pack of Trojans out of the dispensing machine in the men's bathroom.

Arriving at the Shoney's parking lot, we ran into a couple of girls who went to Brainerd High. Rick knew them from junior high school. He set us up for a date for Saturday night to go see a new movie that had recently come out, *Butch Cassidy and the Sundance Kid*.

Saturday night, Rick picked me up in his old Dodge and off we went to get the girls. The first stop was a tour around Shoney's. Then we headed to the theater. The movie was great.

It starred Paul Newman, Robert Redford, and Katherine Ross. After the movie, where did we go? Where else? Shoney's! The date was okay, but I could take or leave Shoney's. I believed there were better places to meet girls.

At any rate, I'd connected with another friend. Still, I knew there were more connections to make.

Chapter 7

A New Name

On Friday nights, I never missed a City High football game. Sometimes I went with friends; other times I accompanied E. Blaine. My dad liked attending all sporting events and he really liked football. Even though I couldn't play, I wanted to cheer on the Dynamos and size up next year's competition.

I met more and more kids and I was becoming more comfortable at school, but I still hadn't found "my" group. One day while eating lunch in the Commons, I sat down at a table with three guys—a couple I had some classes with and one I hadn't met, Marc Williams. He was friendly and I found out he was from North Chattanooga. As I got to know him, it seemed like he knew everyone in school. He was also a Civitan, which meant he was on Miss Pryor's blacklist, and he ran track, specializing in the hurdles. I had run track my sophomore year at Castle Heights. I was a sprinter and ran the 100- and the 220-yard dash. I'd even won a couple races. I earned a letter in track, so Marc and I had a common interest. I guess Mark was impressed with my running skills or stories and we became good friends. He started calling me Buck. Buck was a common nickname for Buchanan and it was hell of lot easier to go by than Carlton. So I became Buck Buchanan and was on my way to being one of the guys at City High.

Marc and I went to the City game against Bradley County. The Dynamos lost 12 to 9. After the game, I began to rethink my refusal to play junior varsity. That Monday, I went to meet Coach Davis. It was time to bury my ego and start getting ready to play ball next year.

Coach Davis's office was in the football locker room, also known as the "Armory," located under the auditorium. When the school was built, it had an ROTC program and this room was where the rifles were stored. Apparently, the new school didn't have a locker room for the football team, or a stadium on campus for that matter. I guess it showed just how unimportant football was to Chattanooga High School, where ROTC got a room, but the football team didn't. ROTC had been dropped a few years earlier, so now the football team had its own locker room.

I walked into Coach Davis's office and told him I wanted to play on the junior varsity team for the rest of the year.

He told me, "Well, son, you've missed a lot of practice, so you'll have to start at the bottom and work your way up." He paused, then added, "I'm not even sure there's any equipment left. But you can go back to the JV equipment cage and if you can find enough equipment that fits, you can report to practice tomorrow afternoon."

His attitude wasn't very encouraging, but I didn't expect much else.

After about 30 minutes, I found enough parts to put a practice uniform together. The helmet was a plastic shell. On the inside, it had some strapping suspended from the sides and a piece of leather in the crown for head support. Around the sides was padding below and above each ear hole. In the front and the back, a piece of foam was glued to the shell. A two-bar face mask was attached to the left side of the plastic shell with two screws. On the right side, only one screw held the bar, so the bar moved up and down on the right side. Not exactly what I wanted in headgear protection. On top of that, it was about a size too big, but I knew it would have to do.

As far as the rest of the uniform went, the only pants left

were a size 36 and I wore a size 28. Luckily, I found a belt. The hip pads were on a belt with two pieces of plastic on each side and another that covered the tail bone. The year before, I'd worn girdle pads. They were like wearing a pair of shorts with pads built in and were far more comfortable and provided much better protection. The shoulder pads were very old and didn't have a string in the front to lace them together, but I found a shoestring in an old cleat lying on the floor and used it. Thank goodness I had my own cleats.

The next day after class, I headed down to the Armory and got dressed in my practice uniform, which looked like it had been issued by the Salvation Army.

Coach Davis had told me to meet Coach Creed on the baseball field for practice; the varsity practiced down the hill on the football practice field. The running track was also down there. Some days the two teams practiced together; other days they practiced separately. This day, the JV practiced by themselves.

LeBron Creed was a community coach who ran JV practice when it was separate from the varsity. LeBron had played for City High a couple of years earlier. There were about 18 kids at practice and after we did the routine calisthenics, Coach Creed called the team together and announced the next drill, called Bull in the Ring. I was familiar with it, because we'd done it at Castle Heights. It was known as one of those "knock the shit out of you" drills. It must have originated from some coach who got the idea while watching the gladiators fight in the *Spartacus* movie.

One player went into the center of the ring. Then the coach called out a random player, who ran to the center of the ring and tried to knock the "bull" out of the ring or on his butt. If the bull defended his position and stayed in the ring, another player went at him. The bull didn't know which direction the next guy was coming from, so he needed to keep his head on a swivel.

It was time to start. The first guy lasted about two rounds and was knocked out of the ring by a linebacker. The linebacker lasted three rounds before being knocked down by a tight end.

Then it was my turn. I was ready. I took off full speed, hit the end under the chin with a forearm, and knocked him out of the ring. Now I was the guy in the middle.

A fairly large lineman came after me at full tilt, but as he approached, I ducked, hit him just above the knees, and flipped him over me; he landed on his back with the wind knocked out of him and had to be dragged out of the ring. Then another lineman, bigger than the last, came at me at full throttle. I side-stepped him, grabbed him by the shoulder pads, and threw him down to the ground. I continued to defend the center as the coach increased the number of players entering the ring. At times, it seemed like three guys were coming at me at once. Amazingly, I went through the entire team and never got knocked out of the ring or on my butt. Luck, speed, and the desire to prove myself were the keys to my success.

After the Bull in the Ring drill, we ran some plays. I practiced at one of the halfback positions in the "T" formation. Then we lined up for wind sprints. I hadn't run any since last track season, but I was determined to prove my speed. The linemen and the backs were broken up into groups. I ran with the backs and finished first in all ten of the sprints. I'd proven myself, showing my toughness and speed. I was pretty happy with my effort, even if it was with the JV team. I'd gained respect from the players and the coach.

The next day in the Common, I ran into Coach Davis. He greeted me with a smile. Referring to my performance the previous day, he said, "I heard you roughed up the boys yesterday. Keep up the good work, because we're going to need all the help we can get next year."

I replied, "Yes, sir."

I was back in football, but knew it was just the start. If I wanted to play in my senior year, I'd have to prove myself every day from then on.

Chapter 8

A Saturday Night

Saturdays were always welcome. Even though my dad always dreamed up something to keep me busy, such as cutting the grass, raking leaves, clearing out the gutters, chopping wood, or straightening up the garage, I could sleep an hour or so later than on school days. Sometimes if there was a school event, the chore list was reduced or I'd be let off the hook entirely.

By now, I was getting more familiar with the seasonal rituals of the City High students. Most of the clubs had some fundraiser during the year. In the fall, Tri Hi Y Club members were "donut girls," as they sold Krispy Kremes on Saturday mornings. I thought this was a great marketing ploy; after all, who could resist a fresh donut from a cute high-school girl?

The girls sold them door-to-door in the neighborhood or stood in the middle of busy intersections, passing out donuts to, and collecting cash from, passers-by as they stopped for the traffic signals. Of course, the boys knew where their girlfriends or the cutest girls were stationed and made numerous trips by these points of enterprise. The girls wanted them to buy all the donuts, so they could go home, but most of the boys were too cheap or broke to buy a dozen. They just wanted to look and flirt. E. Blaine gave me a short reprieve from my Saturday duties to make a quick donut run. He even handed me the money, as long as I got enough for him.

Saturday afternoons in the fall I generally spent watching football, listening to a game on the radio, or hanging out with friends. My dad had season tickets for the University of Tennessee at Chattanooga (UTC) Moccasins. I'd been attending games with him since I was a young boy. If I didn't have anything else to do on Saturday, I went. I always thought it was quite a treat to watch a game at Chamberlin Field, the old stadium in the center of the campus. The home-side stadium seats were built on the back side of a red-brick classroom building with ivy growing over various parts of the exterior walls. Oak trees lined the road to give the entrance an enchanting setting. The visiting-side stands were similar, built on the back side of a red-brick structure that housed dorm rooms and classrooms. At full capacity, the stadium accommodated about 25,000 fans. Although the team was generally mediocre, it was still fun to go to the games and see the "big kids" play.

But on this particular Saturday night, I was going out with some of the guys. Marc Williams invited me over to spend the night. He lived with his mother; his dad died when he was 12. Like me, he had an older married sister who didn't live at home. So Marc, driving his sister's old "bubble-top" red Volvo, picked me up for a night on the town. The plan was to meet a couple of guys from City at Ray Gorrell's house and make a beer run.

Ray's place wasn't too far from where Mark lived. Ray was also a junior at City and lived in a house by himself. When Marc told me about Ray living alone, I didn't believe it. A junior in high school with his own house? Unreal! We pulled up in front of the house and there was an old gray Rambler sitting out front. Marc told me it was Ray's. It was a small framed house with hardboard exterior siding. Inside it had two bedrooms, a den, and a tiny kitchen. The large porch on the front side came with a swing.

I hadn't met Ray before. He was fairly tall at about 6'2" and weighed about 210. He had black hair, thick dark eyebrows, and a heavy beard for a junior. He sort of resembled Bluto, the cartoon character, in the Popeye comics.

As we began to shoot the bull, I found out that his parents were divorced. He'd been living with his mother, who moved to Florida. She wanted him to finish school in Chattanooga, so he stayed behind in the house. She sent him checks from time to time for living expenses. I was impressed with how clean the house was, but I guessed that since he didn't have anyone to cook and clean, he learned how to take care of these "Mom" duties himself.

Marc and I hadn't been there long when two other guys entered the house, Arch Trimble and Gary Seepe. I hadn't met either of them before, although I had heard of Arch. His father was a successful insurance agent and his grandfather was the county tax assessor. Arch Edward Trimble III was a little shorter than I was, but I could tell he was brash and not lacking confidence. Gary was a neighbor of Arch's.

After introductions, it was time for the beer run. I was real curious to hear the plan, since we were all 17 or younger and the drinking age was 21. It was simple: We were going to Granny's. I wasn't sure what that meant, but I knew I'd soon find out.

Ray didn't go with us, because he had a date. Arch volunteered to drive us in his dad's shiny new Plymouth GTX. The body was a bright metallic blue and the top was white. It had a 440-cubic engine and a four-barrel carburetor. Needless to say, it flew. We headed to Suck Creek at the base of Signal Mountain adjacent to the Tennessee River. In the old days, this area had been known as a moonshining haven.

After about 20 minutes, we pulled up in front of a little white house on the side of the road with a small beer sign hanging on a pole out front. We entered a room that looked like at one time it'd been a living room. It was now full of white waist-high chest-type coolers loaded with beer and liquor.

In the middle of the room stood a little old lady, obviously the infamous Granny. A typical grandmother, she was chubby, with white hair in a bun on top of her head. She wore glasses and was dressed in a green smock-type dress. She smiled a lot, but I couldn't tell if she had teeth or not. My guess was not. There was a little chitchat between her and Marc, but that was it. To my surprise, she never requested ID; she didn't even ask us how old we were. We picked out some Pabst Blue Ribbon, paid her, and off we went. We had the beer.

Next stop: Signal Mountain and a slumber party at some girl's house; several girls in our class were there, two of whom Arch and Marc had gone out with. I soon learned that girls' slumber parties were fairly common, taking place every weekend somewhere, and attracted the boyfriends or wannabes. The magnitude of the party depended on how strict the girl's parents were, if they there at all or out of town. This was a new experience for me. Arch and Marc were in and out of the house, but Gary and I just hung out in the driveway with a few other guys, talking and observing the activities.

We stayed there until sometime around 11:30 p.m., then headed back down the mountain to Ray's house. Arch appeared to be sober as he drove down the mountain, showing off his skills handling the GTX at high speeds. He scared the hell out of me, but proved he was quite a good driver. We got to the bottom in one piece.

Arch was hungry, so before we headed back to Ray's house, we made a stop at the Krystal on Cherokee Boulevard in North Chattanooga. The Krystal was an all-time favorite in Chattanooga, home of the small square burgers that came with a thin slice of beef, chopped onions, a pickle, and mustard. You could get a couple of burgers, an order of fries, and a Coke for just a dollar. After stocking up on Krystal hamburgers, it was back to Ray's.

Instead of continuing on to Marc's to spend the night, he

and I crashed at Ray's. We sat around shooting the breeze while we drank the rest of our Pabst Blue Ribbon. It had been an interesting night. I got to know Granny the bootlegger and Arch Trimble. Little did I know that Arch and I would have a lot of adventures together.

Chapter 9

The Seasons End

Mrs. Johnson was one of the older teachers in the English department. She loved poetry and her favorite was Lord Byron, one of the greatest British poets and a leading figure in the Romantic Movement. So she spoke about him frequently and read at least one of his poems weekly. Among Byron's best-known works are the lengthy narrative poems *Don Juan* and *Childe Harold's Pilgrimage*. He died from a fever in 1824 at the age of 36. When Mrs. Johnson talked about his death, she broke out in tears. Whoever took her class might not learn anything about English, but they sure as hell wouldn't forget about Lord Byron.

One of the favorite tricks to play on her was to put thumbtacks on her chair. As she sat down on them, she screamed, jumped up, and started crying. Through the entire semester, she never discovered the culprit. And I'll take that secret to my grave.

Arch and I began to hang out a lot together. We both liked to have a good time and like me, Arch was planning on playing football the following year. He was out for the current season, having injured his knee, which required surgery. Arch was also intrigued that I'd gone to Castle Heights. He asked me a lot of questions about my time at the military school. The military appealed to him, because his dad had served in the Marines.

I continued to practice with the JV and got to play in four games on Thursdays. The juniors and sophomores who played a quarter or less in a varsity game on Friday were eligible to participate in the next scheduled JV game. Players ineligible to participate in varsity sports, like me, could also play in the

JV games. With this rule, I got to play with some of the varsity guys, like Bill Wilder, Pat Petty, Eddie Steakley, and Mike O'Neil. Although I only practiced with the team for about six weeks, I got to know most of the players. At least the players and the coaches knew who I was. Now I had a foot in the door for my senior year. Since most of the starters on the '69 team were seniors, we had a lot work ahead of us.

After practice, I went home to eat dinner with Irene and Blaine. We watched the nightly news between 6 and 7 p.m. before I did any schoolwork or whatever else I had planned for the night. There were three channels to choose from: channel 3 was the NBC affiliate, channel 9 was ABC, and CBS was on channel 12. My folks usually watched the CBS national news with Walter Cronkite. The Vietnam War generally consumed the headlines on the 30-minute national news. The local favorite was Mort Lloyd, a smooth-talking anchorman for the CBS affiliate. He was completely bald and stared directly into the camera with a stern look as he delivered the 30-minute local news. You had the feeling he was talking directly to you about local politics or newsworthy items in and around Chattanooga or North Georgia.

The local news always carried a few stories about sports. On Friday nights, the local high-school football scores were reported during the 11 p.m. broadcast. But if you really wanted to know about sports, you had to read one of the daily papers, the morning *Times* or the afternoon *Free-Press*, which covered high-school sports in detail.

During football season, most of us followed the University of Tennessee Volunteers and the other teams in the Southeastern Conference. UTC football was also a favorite, being the hometown team.

Even as football season continued, the World Series was

getting a lot of attention. In the 1969 World Series, the New York Mets were taking on the Baltimore Orioles. The O's were heavily favored to win, with a lineup filled with such stars as pitcher Jim Palmer, third baseman Brooks Robinson, and outfielder Frank Robinson. The lowly Mets were a young team, anchored by a group of pitchers, including Tom Seaver, Nolan Ryan, and Jerry Koosman. It was the franchise's first winning season in eight tries. They were proclaimed the "Miracle Mets" after they won the series in five games to accomplish one of the greatest upsets in World Series history.

A couple of weeks later, my dad took me to the UTC game. They were playing Louisiana Tech, undefeated at the time and featuring a national-leading offense with a star quarterback by the name of Terry Bradshaw. Bradshaw put on quite a show, leading the Bulldogs to a 23 to 7 victory over the Mocs.

The City High Dynamos closed out the season with a 42 to 14 a victory over Howard High, finishing with seven wins and three losses, its best record since the late '50s. This was a big deal for a school better known for its marching band than its football team. Coach Davis had done a great job in just his second year on the job by getting the team to play together and building a winning attitude.

Central also ended the season seven and three, but they got invited to play in the Civic Bowl in Tullahoma, Tennessee, whereas the City team stayed home. The goals for the following year were already set: Improve on the record and beat Central.

The 1969 team was a senior-dominated team; the only juniors who saw any regular playing time during the season were Joe Burns, Eddie Roberson, and the kicker John Cooper.

The team captains were Ronnie Robertson and Ken Starling. Ken was one of three black players on the team and I'm sure he was the first black captain in school history. He was a bruising fullback and had a scholarship offer to Indiana. Ronnie was a guard and linebacker who was planning on playing at Alabama.

The fact that Ken was black didn't seem to bother anyone on the football team or in the school. He was a damn good player and took a leadership role in whatever he did. It also showed us something about Coach Davis's coaching philosophy, which was once you were on the field, you were one team. The color of your skin was completely irrelevant.

Of course, not everyone in the South saw it that way.

Chapter 10

The Curfew

In the 1800s, Chattanooga was an industrial island floating in an ocean of agriculture throughout the South. While
there certainly was slavery in this part of Tennessee, it wasn't as
prevalent as it was in the cotton fields in the states farther south.
After the Civil War, slavery was abolished, but black people
struggled for equal rights for the next hundred years.

Things slowly began to change in 1954 after the Supreme
Court's landmark decision about segregation, Brown v. Brown,
but it wasn't until the sixties that the civil rights movement
gained momentum, with the Freedom Riders, marches throughout Alabama, the emergence of Martin Luther King as the
peaceful leader, and the integration of public schools pushing
the crusade forward.

Gone were the days of blacks having to sit in the back of the
bus. Separate public bathrooms and water fountains for whites
and blacks were also a thing of the past. Now blacks could go
freely to any restaurant or hotel—in theory, anyway. Society was
changing, but communities weren't. Blacks still lived with blacks
and whites still lived with whites. Opportunities were slow in
opening up for the blacks and there was still fierce opposition by
some to their progress. In the smaller towns around the South,
it wasn't uncommon to see the Ku Klux Klan, dressed in their
white robes and hoods, marching, passing out pamphlets or even
standing on the side of the road soliciting money for their cause.
Towns around Chattanooga, like Soddy Daisy, South Pittsburgh, and Dunlap, were no exception. While Klan membership
continued to decline, its presence was still felt.

For the most part, Southern schools were segregated until the mid-sixties. Even after desegregation, black kids continued to attend black schools and it was the same for white kids. In Tennessee, black and white public schools played against one another in sports, but it also created tension between the races, because most black schools believed that the referees gave the breaks to the white schools.

By the end of the sixties, the South lumbered toward social equality, but no one expected the changes to happen overnight. For the blacks, of course, it couldn't come quick enough, while for the whites, there was no hurry. Old habits are hard to break.

My father had grown up on a farm where blacks worked right alongside whites. He worked, played, even hunted with black kids. One of his best friends growing up was a black boy named Earnest. They maintained that friendship until the day Earnest died. E. Blaine was all about helping the blacks he knew. He assisted them with legal issues, taxes, getting their kids into college, and just about anything else they needed that he could do. On Saturday afternoons, it wasn't uncommon for one of his black acquaintances to drop by the house and get some legal advice. Yes, he did most of this work pro bono. When my sister was born, a black maid came to work for us to help my mother with the baby. We had a part-time maid until I was about 10. So I'd been around black people all my life. I was raised to respect all people. I guess that's why going to school with black kids seemed like no big deal to me.

After four months attending Chattanooga High, I believed the integration process was going smoothly. A number of black students were very active in leadership roles at the school—in the Student Council, Honor Society, social clubs, and sports teams. It seemed that City High School was ahead of the racial-equality curve.

But this wasn't the case at other schools in town, especially Central and Brainerd. Brainerd's use of the Confederate flag as a school symbol was polarizing. Central experienced racial fighting almost daily. In October, the disturbances peaked at both schools. The Chattanooga City Council, fearing that the violence might spread beyond the schools, established a city-wide curfew for a week, from seven in the evening to seven in the morning for anyone under the age of 21. Liquor stores were required to close during these hours. This was the second curfew the city had put in place in nearly two years; the first was in April 1968 during the riots that followed Martin Luther Kings' assassination.

No school activities could be scheduled after 7 p.m. during the curfew. So high-school football games were moved from Friday night to Friday afternoon. When Chattanooga Mayor A.L. Bender lifted the curfew, he stated, "If trouble erupts, I'm in a position to reinstate the curfew in a minute's notice!" Fortunately, this cooling-off period allowed things to calm down and the schools got back to normal, at least for a while.

Not only the high schools were dealing with the integration issue. Colleges and universities were also struggling with the change. Even some of colleges around the South hadn't moved as far toward desegregation as our high school. The University of Tennessee's football team was the first in the Southeastern Conference to have a black player. Lester McClain became an active player on the Tennessee varsity in 1968. At the end of the 1969 season, Alabama had yet to have a black player on the team. So racial tensions certainly remained in the South. We were just fortunate to have avoided them at City High.

The journey to racial equality would be a long one. But once we reached the destination, it was everyone's hope that the conflict over skin color would be a thing of the past.

Chapter 11

The Deer Hunt

Civil rights weren't the only hot-button issue in those weeks. The Vietnam War continued to rage and the body counts mounted. In mid-November, there was a massive protest in Washington, D.C. While it didn't directly affect us, we couldn't help but see what was going on, because it was on the news every day. Most of us knew guys who'd gone to Vietnam. Martha Killeffer's brother Sambo was there. A talented swimmer, he was one of the first swimmers to get a scholarship to the University of Tennessee. But after about a year, he decided that college swimming wasn't for him, so he dropped out of school, joined the Marines, and was in the action somewhere in the jungles. Martha updated us on how he was doing as she got the news.

Most of us talked from time to time about going to Vietnam. No one wanted to; hell, few of us even knew what the fighting was all about. The news portrayed it as part of the battle against communism. The communists in North Vietnam wanted to take over South Vietnam and the Americans had to prevent that from happening, in order to hinder what was called the Domino Theory. But whether we knew anything about any of that, we all agreed that if we got drafted, we'd go. The closer we got to our eighteenth birthdays, the more we faced the possibility of being shipped off to war. I had only 13 months before I hit that pivotal date.

Thanksgiving rolled around and we had our normal holiday lunch of turkey, dressing, and fixings. This year it was just Mom, Dad and I. My sister spent Thanksgiving at her in-laws' house in Middle Tennessee. We watched football on TV after lunch, then E. Blaine and I went up to the attic for a little target practice. We were going deer hunting that Saturday and E. wanted to sharpen up his aim. He had a target range up in the attic for when he couldn't get to the gun club or the weather was bad. My dad loved guns and he went to the gun club two or three times a month; of course, he always wanted me to go with him. I'd been doing this since I was a small boy, so by now I could shoot about any kind of gun and I was a fairly good shot.

E. Blaine had grown up on a farm where hunting was a common activity. He enjoyed hunting as much as guns. He also believed in the Boy Scout motto: "Always be prepared." So that Friday night, we had to make sure all the guns, ammunition, water, and food were loaded and packed in the Woodpecker. Of course, we had enough provisions to last the entire winter. Though we were only going for a day, it didn't matter; we were ready for anything.

The Woodpecker was a 1956 Willys Jeep station wagon. When my dad had got it from a client, it was in fairly bad shape, but he not only cleaned it up, he totally rebuilt it and painted it blue and white. The Jeep was called the Woodpecker, because on each door, he placed a decal of a cartoon woodpecker with a cigar hanging out of its mouth. It had four-wheel drive and a winch on the front of it. It couldn't outrun a mule with a broken leg, but it would go virtually anywhere without getting stuck. The Woodpecker was a true Southern hunting vehicle.

We had our clothes laid out before we went to bed, because it was going to be an early morning. At three a.m. he woke me up and said, "It's time to go." I got a glass of orange juice as I walked out the back door, with Dad telling me "We'll eat in the woods."

As I walked outside, I noticed the thermometer showed the

temperature to be 27°. Gee, was I excited about going deer hunting at three in the morning and freezing to death. We got in the Woodpecker and headed for a piece of property on the north side of the Tennessee River northwest of Chattanooga near Nickajack Dam. According to my dad, this was a great place to hunt deer. He'd been there three weeks earlier with a friend to scout out the trails and look for deer tracks and signs. He now knew where the deer hung out. Supposedly.

It was even colder on the side of the river as we unloaded our gear, ate some tasty beef jerky and a cold biscuit for breakfast, strapped on our backpacks, loaded our rifles, and began our hunt.

After about an hour of hiking up and down hills, we reached a small wooded hilltop that overlooked an open field. I stayed put, while my dad hiked to the opposite side of the hollow; the plan was to trap the deer in the middle. This didn't seem like such a good idea to me, E. Blaine and I on either sides of the valley, shooting at each other. Luckily, there was no sign of a deer; unluckily, I stood at my post for about an hour and my feet were beginning to freeze. My dad returned and we hiked to another spot, where I stood by a tree and waited for deer that obviously weren't destined to die that day. By now it was around 10:30 and E. Blaine was ready to call it quits. A small cheer erupted in my head and I said to myself, "Thank goodness," as my toes were now completely numb. I just hoped the heater in the Jeep worked.

On the way back, we ran across a pile of junk that looked as if it was left over from a fire. There were charred wood, piping, metal tubs, and broken glass. My dad smiled and said, "That was once a moonshine still." Well, okay, we were in Tennessee.

We got back to the house, watched the college football game, and ate dinner. Then Rick Spencer called and wanted me to go to Shoney's to see if we might meet some girls. No surprise, we had the same luck finding two-legged dears as I'd had with the four-legged deer. After a couple of hours, I was ready to head home. I'd had enough hunting for one day.

Chapter 12

Sunday in the Park

Every Sunday morning, we went to Centenary Methodist Church on McCallie Avenue. First came Sunday school, more of a place to socialize than to study the Bible. Most of the 10 or 12 kids in class had been going there since we could remember. Suzanne Miller in the class also went to City; we chatted about the goings-on at CHS.

After Sunday school and before church, I treated myself to a six-ounce bottle of Coke that cost six cents. It was always fun to see what city was on the bottom of the tear-shaped green-glass deposit bottle. Supposedly, the city was the place where the Coke was bottled. I always thought it was cool to get a bottle from a faraway place, such as Houston or Chicago.

After church, we always went out to eat lunch, either at the Town and Country restaurant or the S&W Cafeteria. I preferred the Town and Country, where I'd get my standard cheeseburger with mustard only, fries, and sweet iced tea.

Once home, I changed clothes for our weekly neighborhood game of tackle football, no pads.

The Park was the recreation area in Shepherd Hills, located between Ridgeside and Hilldale roads. The area from the tennis courts on down was somewhat isolated from view, due to the tree line from the yards of the houses that backed up to the Park. The trees provided somewhat of an enclosed area out of the view of the parents. So when the Park wasn't being used for sporting activities, the kids were left up to their own devices, such as smoking, drinking, or whatever.

Whoever showed up and wanted to play was included,

regardless of age or size. Frankly, this is where I learned how to play football. I'd been playing since I was eight or nine years old. Playing the game in the park toughened you up; if the game wasn't tough enough, the obstacles around the field added to the challenge.

The north end zone was the concrete tennis courts. The creek was out of bounds on the left side and the shuffleboard court was out of bounds on the right. The goal line on the south end of the field was between the end of the shuffleboard court and the oak tree on the left side. In the middle of the southern end zone was a jungle gym. The field was about 40 yards at its widest point and about 60 yards long. The out of bounds played into the strategy of the game. You had to watch what you were doing or you'd end up getting tackled into the creek, against a tree, or on the shuffleboard court.

The weekly game had mostly the same guys from the neighborhood playing. Of course, friends were always welcomed. Shortly after two, we chose sides and kicked off.

It was mainly a passing game, but at times, one team or the other tried to imitate the famous Green Bay Packer sweep. This was a challenging play to stop, with five guys leading the charge in front of the ball carrier.

The games lasted an hour and a half or two. They always featured very creative play-calling. The most creative and toughest play to defend was a pass play called "jump-the-net post pattern." When a team was moving toward the northern end zone (at the tennis courts), a receiver ran straight down the field and broke off on a slant toward the center of the tennis court in the end zone, then jumped the net just as the quarterback threw the ball. The defender was always screened off by the net, but sometimes the receiver didn't clear the net completely; he'd catch his foot and nose dive into the concrete court. It was an effective play, but also dangerous. Surprisingly, there were very few serious injuries in our games. It was always a fun time. Winning was always important; it gave you bragging rights for a week.

After the games, we sat around and talked about what happened in the school games on Friday or what the Vols did the day before. The Tennessee Volunteers finished the 1970 season at 9 and 1. They won the Southeastern Conference championship and were scheduled to play Florida in the Gator Bowl.

It was a short walk home. Sunday nights I watched "The Ed Sullivan Show" and did all the homework I hadn't done week before.

Chapter 13

Christmas Time

As Christmas was approaching, the Civitans conducted their annual fruitcake sale. One of the school's most popular fundraisers, most parents seemed to like it, probably because it was a Christmas tradition or it supported a good cause. I really never understood why; to me it was terrible. The fruitcake was made with dried fruit, molasses, nuts, and preservatives in one-dollar bars that were two inches square and about eight inches long. It was very dense and had the consistency of a rubber tire. It was said that as long as a cake was wrapped up, it could last for years and still be edible. As tough as it was, I was sure it could withstand a nuclear blast.

In early December, the Altamont Free Concert was held at the Altamont Speedway in northern California. It was hosted by the Rolling Stones and marketed as "Woodstock West." The media reported on the heavy use of drugs, along with violence perpetrated by Hells Angels hired as security. While this event got a lot of national recognition on the network news, students at our school didn't seem to pay much attention to it. As far as I could see, drugs weren't much of an issue at City High. Some kids smoked pot from time to time at a party or in the parking lot and occasionally someone's locker was searched for marijuana based on a "tip," but hard drugs were mostly unheard of. I'm sure our school administrators credited the low drug activity to the monthly assembly programs about how bad drugs were.

I'd been around weed. I was first exposed to it at the Park in Shepherd Hills, where some of the kids sat around the playground area, smoking a joint and dreaming they were at Woodstock or another rock festival.

The influence of rock 'n' roll and the hippie subculture had also changed the way some teenagers looked and dressed. This look was spreading across the country, but City High remained fairly conservative. The majority of the boys had relatively short hair and wore button-down collared shirts, football jerseys, or T-shirts with jeans. The girls generally wore dresses, skirts, or slacks to class. The mini-skirt was in fashion, so it was also an option. Of course, the boys liked that look!

A few guys grew out their hair and stopped shaving. Their dress consisted of turtlenecks or tie-dyed T-shirts and old jeans. These kids mostly belonged to the People's Club. Some referred to them as the Pot Smoking Club, but there was no evidence of this claim. This group was okay. I was friendly with them; they just weren't the type I wanted to hang out with.

I generally ran around with Arch and Marc. One day after school, Marc had to go to the Martin Thompson Sporting Goods store downtown to pick up some track shoes. I asked him, "Why do you need track cleats in December?"

He said, "I want to break them in before the season starts."

We took off in Marc's sister's bubble-top Volvo. As we pulled up near the store, no parking spaces were available, so Marc said, "You drive the car around the block while I go inside and pick up the shoes."

Well, that was fine, except the Volvo was a stick shift, which I'd never driven before. So here I was, in downtown traffic, in a car I didn't know how to drive. Oh well, how hard could it be?

I tried to take off by hitting the gas and the car died. I got the car started and this time, I tried to use the clutch to shift into one gear or another. I managed to get going and went a couple hundred yards, though obviously in the wrong gear, because the car died. Once again, I got the car started and almost made it around the block. I was making progress. I finally got the gear pattern figured out and was getting a sense of the shifting as I completed my first round-trip to and from the store. I pulled up in front just as Marc came out. He could see that I was freaked out! Of course, all he could do was laugh, saying, "Now you know how to drive a stick shift."

School ended for Christmas and two weeks off. I didn't have much going on during the holidays. I spent my time playing basketball and football, visiting my grandmother in Cleveland, and of course going shopping. Christmas morning, we opened presents, then got ready for Christmas lunch, always a family event. My mother prepared a large traditional meal featuring turkey, dressing, ham, casseroles, deviled eggs, and desserts. My sister Betty and her husband Johnny came down to spend a couple of days. My grandmother joined us on Christmas day; my cousins Connie, Mary Lynn, and Uncle Conrad came by as well. As usual, Uncle Bill wouldn't miss a free meal.

My crazy Uncle Bill was the youngest of my mother's brothers. A painter by profession, he had a fondness for alcohol. Bill was always entertaining, regaling us with his latest exploits on the jobs or with the people he met during his day-to-day activities. Every Christmas, he told us he was going to quit painting and open up a grocery store—this from a guy who didn't have enough money to pay the light bill, but at least he had high ambitions. Frankly, I wasn't sure if Bill was really crazy or just always under the influence of alcohol and paint thinner.

Of course, Uncle Conrad and my cousins asked me how I liked going to City High. I told them I liked it and had met a lot of kids. Uncle Conrad let me know that he hadn't heard anything bad about me from his fellow faculty members, though he hadn't heard anything good either. No news was good news for my mother.

After lunch, we were all entertained by Uncle Conrad's 200 slides of his recent trip to the Holy Land. Naturally, I acted like I really enjoyed the slide show. I figured it was smart to stay on his good side in case I needed an ally at school.

A couple days after Christmas, Tennessee played Florida in the Gator Bowl. The Vols had hoped to go to the New Year's Day Sugar Bowl, but they'd lost to Mississippi earlier in the year, relegating them to the less prestigious Gator Bowl. They were heavily favored to win the game, but ended up losing 14 to 13. Previously, the Gator coach, Ray Graves, had announced that he would retire after the game.

On the 29th of December, I turned 17. One thing you learn early in life when you have a birthday near Christmas is that you only get only one set of presents for both events. Gee, I considered it a real treat to get a cake on my birthday.

New Year's Eve, I spent the night with Arch. He picked me up and we headed to Granny's to get stocked up on beer and vodka. We stopped by a couple of parties and ended our New Year's Eve tour at Ray's. It seemed like that we always ended up at Ray's bachelor pad. Let's face it: It was great thing to have a friend with his own house.

We had a new decade in front of us.

Chapter 14

The '70s are Here

As we woke up the next morning, a little groggy from the New Year's celebration, the '60s were behind us. What a decade it had been! The Cold War had been a major part of the past ten years. The threat of communism drove the politics of the day. The struggles between the United States and the Soviet Union had teetered on the brink of nuclear war, for which the country tried to prepare. Bomb shelters were constructed throughout the country in office buildings, hospitals, schools, and even individual homes. Evacuation drills became part of everyday life in America.

The assassinations of three prominent leaders left a mark on the '60s. President John F. Kennedy had been assassinated in 1963. Civil rights leader Martin Luther King Jr. was shot at a motel in Memphis, Tennessee, in April 1968. Two months later, John Kennedy's brother Bobby was gunned down in California while campaigning for the presidency.

The Beatles led the "British invasion" of the U.S. in 1964. Their impact had been one of the catalysts of change in the country, not the least of which was music moving from bebop to acid rock. The introduction of the birth-control pill in 1965 gave women the kind of sexual freedom they'd never experienced before. With the military involvement in Vietnam, GIs had returned to the States experienced in exotic drugs from hash to heroin. The slogan "sex, drugs, and rock and roll" came out of the '60s, but it was alive and well into the '70s. Otherwise, we didn't know what to expect from the new decade, except that the social changes would continue.

Over the next ten years, we'd also be faced with dramatic changes in our personal lives—perhaps the biggest change in a ten-year period in our lifetime. Most of us would graduate from high school, then go to college or the military, or get a job; some would get married and start a family, and almost all of us would start our working careers. In short, we'd be grown up by the end of the '70s. The days of sports, cheerleading, double-dating, underage drinking, summer fun, etc. would just be a memory. Hell, we didn't have much time left, so we wanted to enjoy the remaining time in high school and not worry about the future until we had to!

New Year's Day was always devoted to watching the four big bowl games. The Cotton Bowl started things off, with Texas beating Notre Dame 21 to 17. The Sugar Bowl featured Ole Miss against Arkansas; Archie Manning led the Rebels to victory in the New Orleans game. In the Rose Bowl, Coach John McKay led his USC Trojan team to an undefeated season by beating Michigan 10 to 3. The final game of the day, the Orange Bowl, ended with a Penn State win over Missouri. At the end of the day, Texas was crowned as the national champion.

My mother always thought that on New Year's Day, you had to have a good lunch. So in the middle of the ballgames, we had to break for cornbread, turkey, ham, collard greens, and black-eyed peas—the special meal to kick off the year. My mother always told me that I needed to eat the black-eyed peas to bring good luck for the New Year. As much as I detested those nasty little peas, I preferred to expect bad luck for the year!

School started back on January 5. The winter sports picked up after the Christmas break. As for me, it was time to get focused on school and to catch up on the work that was due at the end of semester in three more weeks.

Marc had been dating Gigi Galbraith, who played on the girls' basketball team. She wanted Marc to come watch her play. He didn't want to go by himself, so he asked me if I'd go with him. I said, "Sure." I'd never seen a girl's high school basketball game. I thought it might be interesting. Also, I'd recently met a couple other girls on the team, Karen McNichols and Becky Dillender, so it would be fun to see them in action.

The girls' game was quite different than the boys'. The boys played normal basketball, five-on-five full-courts. The girls' teams started six players. It was a three-on-three half-court game, with three guards and three forwards. The guards played defense and guarded the basket, but were not allowed to cross the half-court line. The three forwards played offense and did all the scoring. Like the defenders, they couldn't cross the half-court line. The guards got possession through turnovers or rebounds and could dribble up to the half-court line, but there they had to pass it to one of the forwards on the other side of the half-court line. After watching it for a while, we got the hang of the game.

During a time-out, Gigi came over to the bench, saw Marc in the stands, and gave him a big smile. After the time-out, the game resumed. Gigi grabbed a rebound and started dribbling up court as fast as she could. As she neared the half-court line, she lost her balance and fell down flat on her face. She wasn't hurt, other than a floor burn on her chin—and the embarrassment of stumbling in front of her boyfriend.

City High's team had one player, Sharon Cable, who was unbelievable. She was a forward and could make any shot from anywhere in the half-court area. She also handled the ball like a boy basketball player. Hell, the way she played, she could have been a starter on the boy's team. In addition to basketball, she was a star volleyball player.

My acquaintance Becky Dillender also played offense. She had a good shot, but Sharon got the most opportunities to score.

The girls' team was coached by Claude Catron, who was also one of the football coaches, and he built the offense around Cable. Karen McNichols and Gigi were guards and played defense. Without a doubt, Sharon was the star of the team. As Sharon went, so did the girl's team.

The game had been fun and got me in the mood for winter workouts for football, which started the following week. I was curious to see how Coach Davis ran them. Some of the guys said they were tough and others said they were a piece of cake. I'd find out soon enough.

Chapter 15

Winter Workouts

With professional basketball in full swing, the NFL football season officially ended with the fourth Super Bowl. For the second year in a row, a former AFL team, the Kansas City Chiefs, beat an old NFL team, the Minnesota Vikings. The score was 23 to 7. The AFL had done something that few people thought would happen: They proved they were at least equal to the NFL on the field. Now, after four Super Bowls, each league had won two games.

The next day at school, the big game was the talk on the Commons and at the cafeteria. Marc and I were eating lunch when one of the cheerleaders came by to visit. Marc introduced me to Sheron Bunch. She was one of the cutest girls at City, with dark hair, big brown eyes, and a big smile. On top of that, she had a bubbly personality. We talked for a short while, then it was time for class. The whole time, I was thinking, Okay, I'm in love! After she left, Marc told me that she knew everyone in school, she was everybody's favorite girl, and she was dating Randy S. Gray, a pitcher on the baseball team. Oh well, so much for love at first sight.

Another girl who caught my eye was Kathy Huffaker, a cute blond. It wasn't long before I found out that she'd been dating Bill Wilder, a junior quarterback who lived on Signal Mountain. He had played in a couple of the varsity games last season and even scored a few touchdowns. I'd gotten to know him through fall practice. Bill was always a friendly guy and we talked about getting ready for winter workouts.

The first day of the workouts, 40 or 50 of us reported to the Armory. The Armory was also where the wrestling team worked out, so there were mats on the floor, plus padding over the concrete walls that abutted the mats. There was also a new weight machine, which had numerous stations for a variety of weight exercises, ranging from the bench press to squats.

Coach Davis outlined what to expect over the next two months: three days a week lifting weights and two days a week of general activities like wrestling and, weather permitting, we'd go outside to run and throw the ball around.

Then we got the "speech." You know, every football coach has to give speeches; it's just part of the job. He said, "Boys, if you want to have a winning record and improve over last year, it starts today. If you want to beat Central, it starts today. If you want to play next fall, it starts today. If you want to be successful, you have to work at it. The harder you work, the better you get. If you want to play on Friday nights, you have to work hard during the week. To win, you have to play together and be a team. I don't care who your daddy is or who your girlfriend is or where you live. I don't care if you like each other outside this room or not, but when you walk through these doors and you're out on the field, you are all one. We are all a team. Teams win, not individuals! Do you understand?"

A loud chorus of "Yes, sir!" rang out.

He paused and surveyed the room with a piercing look. Each one of us got the feeling that he was staring straight at us, and then he said, "Now let's get to work. And remember, if it doesn't hurt, it doesn't help."

We all cheered and scurried off to our assigned stations to work with the weights.

I'd never lifted before. Surprisingly, we didn't lift weights at Castle Heights. The only heavy-object workout I'd ever done was lifting bricks and blocks in our backyard at home, where we had a stack of 300 or 400 red-clay bricks. Each summer, E. Blaine gave me the assignment to move that stack of bricks. I guess he thought that it was a good way to keep me occupied and out of trouble. So starting at the young age of six, each summer I moved the stack from the front of the backyard to the back of the backyard. The next year, I moved it back to the original location. Once I got to be a teenager, he bought a couple of pallets of concrete blocks, so I got to move them in addition to the bricks. I guess he figured I needed more weight to carry. Until now, moving masonry products was the extent of my weightlifting.

On the days when we had activities, we wrestled. A better description might be controlled fighting. Anything was legal, except kicking and hitting with a fist. Coach Davis loved to pit a small back against a big lineman. Since I was a back, at first I thought this was intimidating, but I found out that it wasn't all that bad. Typically, the linemen were much slower, so my strategy was simple: I just stayed away from them and hoped they didn't fall on me. When it was time to get aggressive, I hit them just below the knees and they fell like a chopped-down oak tree. Once they hit the deck, I could jump on top of them before they could move and pin them down. I always seemed to get paired up with David Paterson, better known as Chug. He weighed at least 270 pounds and if he landed on me, it would certainly hurt. Luckily, I was just too quick for him and never got crushed.

Bill Wilder also got to go against the big linemen. One match pitted him against a tackle. The tackle got hold of Bill and wouldn't let go, so Bill bit him. Later that week, the tackle's mother called Coach Davis, upset that the coach would allow such a thing. "You realize a bite could cause an infection," she warned. The coach assured her that there would be no more biting at the winter workouts. So the next time we had wrestling activities, Davis told us, "No more biting—unless it's absolutely necessary."

Sometimes while we were lifting weights, the wrestling team was practicing on the mats. This gave me an opportunity to watch and to get to know some of those guys. One was Pat Petty, whom I'd met the previous fall during football practice, but didn't know well. He was about my size and played guard and nose tackle. He wrestled as a way to build strength and increase his quickness for football. As I got to know Pat, I found out that he was very intense when it came to football, or anything else for that matter. He also expected you to prove yourself before he accepted you as a friend or teammate.

After fully recovering from knee surgery, Arch was now working out with the team. There were a couple other guys that were at winter workouts I hadn't met before, because they were recovering from injuries or hadn't played in the fall. Tommy Richmond, a junior guard, had also recently recovered from knee surgery. He was friendly and when he got excited, he had little bit of a stutter. He grew up in Rivermont and the guys who'd known him since elementary school would sometimes give him a hard time about his stuttering. He seemed to take it in stride and he was always able to give back whatever was given to him.

Marvin Day, a sophomore linebacker, was also beginning to work out with the team. He too had a knee injury that kept him off the field the previous season. He was a friend of David Soloff's, whom I'd met during football practice. He was a guard and linebacker. Both lived on Signal Mountain. David was friendly and always seemed to have a big smile on his face. Marvin, on the other hand, seemed to be kind of serious.

The last week of January was devoted to first-semester finals, so no workouts were scheduled. This marked the end of my first semester at CHS. In a week or so, we'd know our grades. During that week, rumors started going around about some big changes with the football program at Central High.

Chapter 16

Big News from Central

Hey, I passed all my classes and it was the start of a new
semester.

Eddie Francisco didn't have to worry about passing his
classes. He was one of those smart guys. He was also president
of the Honor Council. And he was somewhat of a legend from
junior high. One day in 1966 at Northside Junior High while he
was sitting in class, a workman working on the roof fell through
a skylight and landed right on top of Eddie. He suffered a frac-
tured skull and almost died. Pat Petty was sitting right behind
him. Eddie always thought that Petty was the intended victim,
but cosmic forces conspired against him that day. He'd lost two
pints of blood by the time the ambulance arrived. He spent the
rest of the year homebound, tutored by a new graduate from
UTC. Of course, Eddie developed a crush on her and wanted
to marry her. It took him several months to fully recover. The
accident was well-known in North Chattanooga. One day in
high school, Eddie aced a test and the teacher asked him if the
man falling on his head was the reason why he was so smart.
Francisco just rolled his eyes and thought, "Sure, it's called the
trauma-room approach to acquiring intelligence." Well, not all
of our teachers were Phi Beta Kappa's.

As the new semester started, I recognized a new guy in the
halls, Louie Card. I'd known him since nursery school. He was
now going to City after stops at Baylor and Sewanee Military
Academy. Louie said he was glad to be out of the military
schools. I knew exactly how he felt.

And there was big news out of Central High School. After

27 years, Coach Red Etter was leaving the school to coach at The Baylor School for Boys. Wow! This was a shock to the entire city.

There was a lot of speculation as to why he'd make such a change after all those years. Publicly, Coach Etter never gave a reason for the move, but most thought it was due to Central moving to its new location earlier in the year. The coach lived in the Red Bank area, just a stone's throw from Baylor, whereas the new Central was a 30-mile drive one way. Another factor may have been that his eldest son, Gene, was a teacher and coach at Baylor. Whatever the reason, this move would change Chattanooga's high-school-football landscape.

During his tenure at Central, Coach Etter never lost to a City High football team. His Central teams won seven state championships. What made him such a good coach was that, like all good coaches, he believed in hard work. But more important, he was innovative. He was one of the first high-school coaches to use film to analyze his opponents and find their weaknesses, as well as to evaluate his own team in order to make improvements. He was open to new ideas. He liked changing formations and trying new plays. He started out coaching using the single-wing formation, then went to the "T" formation and then on to the power "I". His teams rarely made mistakes during games. One more advantage was that he could get the best players, all of whom wanted to play for a winner.

Red Etter wasn't just a great football coach. He was also a teacher who managed a full class load ranging from history and Latin to math.

Now, with their great coach gone, what would the Purple Pounders do? There was no time-line for his replacement, so most likely there would be no announcement until school was out.

More home-state football news came out that same week. Coach Doug Dickey was leaving the University of Tennessee for the head coaching job at the University of Florida. While this was disappointing, it didn't come as a great surprise, since he'd played football there. Tennessee was quick to replace him by hiring Bill Battle, a young coach already on the staff. Battle played football for Bear Bryant University of Alabama. Gee, how was this going to work? An arch-rival coaching the Vols? Time would tell.

Although there was a lot of news about football, the basketball season was in full swing. City's boys' basketball team was supposed to be good this year, but they were off to a slow start. Little did we know that they were on the verge of shocking the local basketball world.

Chapter 17

A Streak Ends

On days when there were basketball games or wrestling matches, we were sometimes allowed to get out of winter workout early. On this particular day, there was a game between City and Riverside. City's team was struggling with a losing record, while Riverside, an all-black school, was a powerhouse that hadn't lost in 66 games over a span of three years. Dorsey Sims, the Riverside coach, had won two consecutive state championships and a third was in his sights. Everyone expected Riverside to run all over hapless City. The game was at Riverside High on 3rd Street, the home of Chattanooga High for almost 60 years. When City moved to its present location in North Chattanooga, Riverside moved onto the old CHS campus.

We didn't have a scheduled workout on the day of the big game. When I met Chris Boehm and Martha Killeffer in the parking lot for the ride home, Chris said, "Let's go to the game."

I was riding with them, so I said, "Sure," even though I was thinking, "Are we nuts?" White kids going to a game at a black school? Oh well, just another adventure in life.

The gym was decades old. One of the wood backboards looked like it had a bullet hole in it, but I convinced myself that it was just where the white paint had worn off. Around the gym floor were built-in wooden benches. Hanging from the rafters were the two state-championship banners.

As we entered the old arena, there was already a large loud crowd. The JV teams had just finished playing. By varsity game time, the gym was packed. The majority of the spectators were obviously Riverside fans. Only about 30 or so white fans were in the stands. Of those 30, a handful were students; I happened to be one of those.

We sat near half-court. The teams were just finishing up their warm-up drills. Riverside looked like a college team the way they ran the drills, plus three or four of them had to be seven feet tall. The team, the crowd, and the banners hanging above created an intimidating atmosphere. And that was from the stands. I could only imagine what our players were thinking.

City had only two black players, LeBron Crayton and Wayne Ellison. The stars of the team were senior forward Randy Russell and junior guard Mark Eaton. When they got hot, they could shoot the lights out. Creighton, Rick Rhodes, Allen Brooks, and Kenny Smith all got playing time and every now and then, Eddie Steakley would get to play. The team was coached by Jim Phifer, the assistant principal.

Steakley was a talented athlete from North Chattanooga. He was about six-five and about weighed 230 pounds. He could certainly hold his own on the court. He'd been playing street ball since he was very young. During the summers, Eddie and a couple of his buddies got up games wherever they could and played for money. He wasn't afraid to go into the black communities to challenge black kids to a game of two on two or three on three. Whatever the game, his team almost always won. He just knew how to play. So the Riverside environment didn't intimidate him in the least.

Steakley was a character, to say the least, and it always seemed that he was in or just out of Coach Phifer's doghouse. So far this year, he hadn't played very much. But Phifer must've had a sixth sense about Steakley. He was somewhat of a magician, not so much in handling the ball, but the way he played the game. He knew how to get position for rebounds whether on offense or defense. He also knew the tricks. He was an expert at holding a player's jersey, stepping on toes, and even spitting on opponents without them knowing where it came from. This got his opponent mad and gave Eddie an advantage. Amazingly, he could do all these things without being caught by the referees.

Steakley didn't start the game, but it didn't take long for Phifer to put him in. I was thinking that he might just be City's secret weapon this afternoon. And the momentum did begin to change. By the start of the second quarter, it was obvious that some of the Riverside players were getting pissed off at Eddie's style of play. They yelled at the referee over Eddie holding their jerseys as they went up for rebounds, but the ref never seemed to see anything.

The lead went back and forth.

About midway through the third quarter, City had taken control of the game.

You can imagine the tension in the air, with the 66-game winning streak in jeopardy. Not to mention that Riverside might lose to a white team.

Several Chattanooga policemen were stationed around the arena. During one timeout while Riverside was down, a Riverside fan came on to the court and was headed toward one of the referees. Perhaps he'd seen a few too many of Steakley's holding tricks that hadn't been called and wanted to talk to the ref about it. Fortunately, before he reached the ref, the police went into action and quickly escorted the man out of the facility without further incident.

As the fourth quarter started, City began to falter and the lead seesawed back and forth. Senior forward Randy Russell's outstanding shooting and Steakley's defensive play against Riverside's All-State forward Ed Woods kept the Dynamos in the game. During the fourth quarter, it seemed like Russell couldn't miss, hitting from all over the court. Unfortunately, Riverside was matching him shot for shot.

Down the stretch, LeBron Crayton hit a couple of clutch free-throws, despite the deafening taunting and jeering from the crowd. It was evident that the Riverside fans didn't like a white team beating them, but they really didn't like a black kid playing for a white team. They gave him hell by calling him Uncle Tom and Oreo, but LeBron didn't let it affect his play.

As the clock ticked down, the game was tied. City had the ball driving toward the basket. With two seconds on the clock, senior guard Allen Brooks was fouled as he was passing the ball. He went to the foul line to shoot a one and one. If he hit the first shot, the game was over. The Riverside fans made a tremendous noise that somehow intensified as Allen readied to shoot. He launched the ball and it missed the goal, the net, and all—a total air ball! The game was going to overtime.

The teams traded goals though out overtime as the lead went back and forth. In the final seconds, City took the lead, then held on to win the game 60 to 58.

The 66-game winning streak had come to an end.

The thrill of victory by the City High team and the couple dozen fans was brief. After a few minutes of exuberance, we realized where we were. That was about the same time the Riverside fans overcame their shock and disappointment; some turned angry and tensions were high.

Chattanooga's finest came on to the court and rounded up the 30 white fans, the referees, and the City players, then ushered us all to the locker room. Martha, Chris, and I were relieved, since our car was parked a fairly good ways from the gymnasium.

We could hear the yelling from outside; people were also beating on the door.

As the fans, players, and coaches crowded in the locker room, I found myself standing next to Kenny Smith, who'd played a good bit of the game. I hadn't spoken to him since the first week of school when he acted like he'd never seen me before. I told him, "Good game, Kenny."

He said, "Thanks, Buck."

Talking about the game, the ice between us was now broken. His memory had come back.

We stayed in the locker room for about an hour and a half and were then escorted by the police to our cars one group at a time.

What an exciting game and experience! We were on the verge of being right in the middle of a race riot. We didn't know what we were more thankful for: City winning the ballgame or getting out of the gym alive! The Riverside game was just what the basketball team needed; they would win the next 11 games. But Riverside would get its revenge at a game played at City High School, which they won by four.

When I finally got home the night of the game, my mother was worried sick, but E. Blaine wanted to know all about the game. He didn't say it, but I knew he wished he'd been there.

The Riverside game had been Steakley's high-school basketball-career coming-out party. He had developed a reputation as a very good player from his days at Northside Junior High, but until now, he hadn't been able to get on the court. The question was, could he continue to play at this level and be committed to the team? We'd soon find out.

Chapter 18

An Early Exit

One of the big school events was Stunt Night. Sponsored by the *Dynamo*, the school yearbook, it was a variety show in which many students demonstrated their talents in music, dance, stunts, and a variety of skits. The 1970 edition was titled "The Many Sounds of Now." It was also the time when Miss CHS was announced.

Miss CHS was a tradition going back almost 50 years. The winner, Jeannie Hattenbach, was selected from a group of nine senior girls. Jeannie was a varsity cheerleader, a member of Tri Hi Y and the Honor Society, and a Leo Calendar Girl, and she was naturally very popular.

The basketball season was winding down. I was now a member of the "Troop," a bunch of boys, mostly Civitans, who sat together during the basketball games and cheered on the Dynamos, using nonstandard cheers, such as: "Motorboat, motorboat, putt, putt, putt, we have a team that will beat your butt." Foster Yates and Marc headed up the cheering group and were normally joined by Chip Allen, Marvin Smith, and others.

With only three games remaining on the schedule before the district tournament, Steakley got caught for smoking in the school bathroom. Coach Phifer had no choice but to kick him off the team. Eddie was having a good season and was even getting some interest from colleges. Steakley's parents wanted to keep this interest alive, hoping for a scholarship offer. They asked for a meeting with the coach.

The Steakleys along with Eddie showed up at Coach Phifer's office and asked Phifer to give Eddie another chance.

After some discussion, the coach agreed to let him back on team, under three conditions: no more skipping classes, extra wind sprints and line drills after practice, and if he got caught smoking one more time, he'd be gone for the rest of the year. All parties agreed, Eddie's parents departed, and Eddie appeared to be headed back to class.

About five minutes after the meeting, Phifer left his office, saw Kenny Smith in the hall, and asked him to go with him.

Kenny asked, "Where are we going, Coach?"

"We're going to catch Steakley smoking and you're going to be my witness."

They walked up the east hall, entered the boys' bathroom, and there, just five minutes after vowing not to smoke, was Eddie Steakley, lit cigarette in his mouth and caught red-handed. Needless to say, he didn't play any more basketball that year. It was not only bad for Eddie, but it hurt the Dynamos in the district.

The basketball team was going into the district tournament as the top seed with high expectations to go far into the state playoffs. They'd won four of their last five games. City was playing Brainerd in the first round of the single-elimination tournament. This should have been an easy game for the Dynamos, who'd beaten Brainerd three times earlier in the year. However, it wasn't the Dynamos' night. From the tip-off, nothing seemed to go right for the maroon-and-white guys. They fell to the Brainerd Rebels by 12, thus ending a promising basketball season.

We all expected the basketball team to get to the regionals and we were looking forward to traveling to see them play, but that didn't work out. On the other hand, the wrestling team had done well and had a number of wrestlers going to the state tournament in Nashville. I wasn't as interested in wrestling as I was in basketball, but I allowed myself to be talked into going to Nashville. Sure, I wanted to support the team, but I'd also heard Nashville was a fun place for unchaperoned teenagers.

Chapter 19

Road Trip

By now, Arch Trimble and I were big buddies. When we weren't at school or winter workouts, I was at his house. I probably spent more time at his house than I did at mine. Sometimes after school, we played basketball in his driveway on his eight-foot goal. Depending on how many kids we had, we split into teams and played for hours. The short basket made us feel like we were playing in the NBA—we could all dunk the basketball or shoot from anywhere on the court. The games were very competitive and a lot of fun.

Arch and I made plans to attend the wrestling tournament, to be held in Nashville on a Friday and Saturday. Imagine our surprise when it was announced at assembly that anyone who actually went to the tournament would be excused from school on Friday. That clinched it; we'd get out of school for a day and take a road trip. Several other kids were going up for the meet, including Marc and Gary Seepe, who'd decided to go with us. Friday morning we took off in Arch's blue GTX. Of course, before we hit the road, we had to make a stop at Granny's and stock up on beer.

After our beer was secured, we got on I-24 and headed for Music City. Arch was driving and I was sitting in the front seat. He asked me to open the glove compartment to get out his sunglasses. When I opened it up, sitting inside was a loaded 22-caliber pistol. I was somewhat shocked and asked him, "Did you know you had a pistol in here?"

He said, "Sure, I always keep it in there. Hell, you never know when it might come in handy."

I thought, "Is that a good thing or a bad thing?" I handed him the glasses and shut the compartment door. I learned something new about Arch all the time.

With that surprise behind me, Arch popped an eight-track tape in the tape player. "Born To Be Wild" by Steppenwolf blared out of the speakers as we rocked down the road. The intention was to save the beer until we got to Nashville, but as we passed South Pittsburgh, Marc determined that it was time. He cracked open a cold Pabst Blue Ribbon. We all joined him and toasted our trip and the good times ahead.

The speed limit on the interstate in Tennessee was 75 miles an hour, which meant most people cruised at about 85 in normal traffic. The interstate from South Pittsburgh to Monteagle Mountain was fairly straight, so Arch showed us how fast the car would go. We were cruising at 90 when he floored it, and in just a few seconds we were up 150 miles an hour. He peaked at about 155 mph, then dropped back to a cruising speed of about 125, until we got to the base of the mountain. Arch really liked to drive fast.

Our trip to Nashville was relatively quick, with Arch averaging around 100 miles an hour. Upon arrival in the state capital, we went straight to the Andrew Jackson Hotel in downtown, not far from the Capitol. We picked the Andrew Jackson for two reasons: E. Blaine told me it was an okay place to stay and it was fairly cheap; and a number of our schoolmates were staying there as well.

Upon arrival, it appeared that the Andrew Jackson Hotel was built when Andrew Jackson himself was president in the 1830s and little had been done to update it since. In other words, it was old and rundown, but it was cheap!

We unloaded our gear, iced down the beers, and took off for the wrestling tournament at Hillwood High just outside

Nashville. We watched several matches that a couple of our schoolmates won and qualified for the next day.

We went to dinner with several other kids from school. All the junior cheerleaders were there. I sat between Susan Massey and Sheron Bunch. I found Sheron fun to be around and learned that we both had grandparents who lived in Cleveland, Tennessee.

The Andrew Jackson was fairly near Printers Alley. We'd all heard that it was kind of a mini New Orleans. Of course, none of us had been to New Orleans, but we were well aware of its reputation as a party town.

Printer's Alley was one of the nightclub districts that dated back to the 1940s. At the beginning of the 20th century, it was home to a thriving publishing industry, thus the name. As the publishing business began to transition out, nightclubs and entertainment establishments opened in its place. Nashville musicians often frequented these clubs after work; some of them got their start playing for tips in these joints.

After strolling the narrow streets of Printer's Alley from one end to the other, we developed a plan as to how we could get into one of the bars. The drinking age in Tennessee was 21 years old, we were all just 17, none of us looked any older than our age, and we didn't have any fake IDs. So we decided to give one of the cabaret joints a try. They had a cover charge to get in. Our theory was that if we paid the admission fee, they wouldn't care how old we were.

The cover charge, $3, was posted on the door. As we approached, the bouncer who was collecting the money gave the four of us a look like, who are you kidding? But then he said, "Five dollars apiece."

Well, none of us said a word. We each just handed him an Abe Lincoln and walked in. Since we'd never been in a place like this before, we thought $5 was a bargain.

A four-foot stage stood in back of the room just opposite the front door. A maroon curtain trimmed in gold hung from ceiling to floor about six feet from the front edge of the stage. Tables and chairs were set around the center and on the right side. On the left side was a bar that ran the whole length of the wall. The place wasn't very crowded, so we took a table on the right side of the room. We didn't want to be the center of attention. We hadn't been seated long when a waiter came up to us and asked if we wanted to order something. Wow, they were letting us drink! We all ordered beers, which were $2.50 apiece. At a price like that, we couldn't afford to drink too many, so we were nursing them as the music started to play and the curtains opened.

Two ladies strutted onto the stage. They came out wearing lacy dresses hemmed below their knees and carried two large feather fans. They wore a lot of makeup with bright red lipstick. No spring chickens, they might have been older than our mothers. Nonetheless, we felt like big shots. We were in a Nashville cabaret drinking beer and enjoying the moment.

The dancers paraded around the stage to the beat of the jazz music that came from a three-man band near the left side of the stage. As the show went on, the ladies began to remove their clothing, though they were behind their feather fans, now fully opened on a stand. Protected by the feather "screen," they removed an article of clothing, tossing it up in the air. After about 15 minutes, they were down to their underwear. Still, it was hard to see anything except their faces and feet, covered most of the time by the big feather fans. Finally, the music ended, the ladies bowed, the curtains closed, and that was that. It wasn't exactly what we'd envisioned from a cabaret show, so we got up to go.

I'd only brought $40 with me for the whole weekend, which had to cover hotel, meals, gas, and entertainment. The Printers Alley excursion took about a fourth of my budget. The other guys weren't in any better shape, so we went back to the hotel.

As we entered the lobby, we ran into the other City High kids in Nashville for the tournament. Of course, Marc knew them all. I recognized a few of the girls, but not the guys. We invited them up to our room for a little socializing.

As we were getting on the elevator, so were three soldiers who were also staying at the Andrew Jackson. They must have been on leave from Ft. Campbell in nearby Clarksville, Tennessee. It looked like they'd been out to Printers Alley as well and had had too much to drink. We exchanged friendly hellos.

One of them was fairly big, six-three or six-four. He asked us, "Got any girls with you?"

We said, "No."

He replied, "Well, if you did, I'd come to your party."

All we said was goodbye as we got off the elevator and headed to our room. They stayed on, going up to another floor. We hoped we'd had seen the last of them.

About 20 minutes later, the group from City we'd seen in the lobby showed up. There were now about 10 or 12 of us in the room. The black-and-white TV was on and a couple of conversations were going about what teenagers talk about when they're together.

About an hour later, around midnight, there was a knock at the door and in walked the loudmouth soldier we'd met on the elevator.

It was obvious that he was much more intoxicated now than he'd been earlier. He went on to tell us that he'd come to join our party and there wasn't anything we could do to stop him, because he had a key that opened every room in the hotel.

I thought: "How in the hell did he get such a key?" But that wasn't the main issue we were faced with. There was only one of him at the time, but we knew he had friends. We felt like the four of us could probably take care of him, but we weren't sure; after all, he was a trained soldier. Naturally, Arch was confident that he could whip the big guy's ass all by himself. Marc and I were a little more cautious.

So here we were with a drunken soldier in our room, threatening us and hitting on some of the girls. We tried to carry on, but we could see it wasn't going well. Private Loudmouth, as we called him, wanted only to talk to the girls and, of course, they were scared to death of him.

I told Marc to keep an eye on Arch, because in situations like this, he could sometimes be a hothead and not use his best judgment. Also, I hadn't forgotten the .22 pistol in his glove compartment.

I did my best to talk to the soldier and convince him that he really didn't want to be in a hotel room with a bunch of high-school kids. Then I asked him to leave. This debate went back and forth for about 15 minutes until finally, he got up to go. But as he left the room, he turned, holding the key in his hand, and said with a big smile, "If I want to come back, oh, I'll come back. Remember, I have the key!" Then he turned and headed to the elevator. Thank goodness!

After another 15 minutes, the other kids were ready to end the party and get the hell out of our room. Marc and I escorted the girls to their rooms. The good thing was that Private Loudmouth didn't know where their rooms were, but he surely knew where our room was. We got back to the room and drank a few beers, while rehashing the encounter.

Before we went to bed, we tried to lock the door. Wouldn't you know it? Our room didn't have a deadbolt or even a safety chain. So we formed a protective barricade by putting anything that wasn't nailed down in front of the door: chairs, a desk, towels, and bags. Apparently, this secured us against our soldier friend.

The next day we went to watch the finals of the state wrestling championship. In the end, City High tied for third in the state and had two state champions: Benton Hood in the 126-pound class and Doug Daily in the 148-pound class. This was an impressive accomplishment for our school and we were all excited about the outcome.

We went to dinner with a group to celebrate the victory. Sheron was with us and I got a chance to talk to her again. From there we took one more walk down Printers Alley. To try something new, we lined up outside a jazz bar. We didn't have to show ID and only had to pay $2 to get in. They must have thought we went to Vanderbilt, because there were a number of "Vandy" students inside. The beers were only a $1, so we drank our fill. About midnight, we headed back to the hotel room. Fortunately, we didn't run into our Army friend, but we barricaded the door again just to be on the safe side.

Sunday morning, we headed back to Chattanooga, arriving mid-afternoon. I crashed on the couch watching pro football. After dinner, I did a little homework and got ready for class the next day.

We'd had a good time in Nashville. Winter sports were over and spring was on its way. That meant spring sports, spring vacation, spring football practice, and spring weather. Unfortunately, a real-life lesson was also coming our way.

Chapter 20

Tragedy Strikes

I was sitting at a table during lunch in the Commons, talking with some guys about the wrestling victories over the weekend, when Sheron approached and said she wanted to talk to me. "I have a friend I'd like you to meet. I think you two would hit it off well. Her name is Cindy."

Of course, I said, "Sure." I supposed that Sheron knew me well enough by now that she wasn't afraid to introduce me to one of her friends.

Sheron replied, "Great. I'll bring her by tomorrow at lunch." I thought, "How cool is this?" I couldn't wait to meet Cindy!

The next day at lunch, Sheron came around with a blond girl and introduced me to her good friend Cindy Frazier.

Cindy and I began to chitchat and I learned that she lived in Brainerd not far from me. We knew several people in common from the area. She'd gone to Brainerd Junior High and lived only two miles from the high school, but attended City, from which her sister Mary and her brother Billy had both graduated, though her other brother David had gone to Brainerd. She said she'd met a number of Mary's friends and liked what they said about City.

We had to cut our conversation short, because it was time to go to a special assembly to celebrate the wrestling team's success. We promised to continue our chat at lunch the next day. She was easy to talk to and I looked forward to getting to know her better.

Spring sports were beginning. Baseball, golf, tennis, and track would get all the attention now. I'd have loved to play baseball or at least run track, but I was still ineligible due to the school-transfer rule. I could, however, participate in spring football and that was only a couple weeks away. I'd been working out for two months and was ready to show what I could do on the varsity football field.

Cindy and I kept bumping into each other in the halls and we always stopped to talk, even if it was only for a minute or two. I was beginning to see that she had a great sense of humor. Gee, I was beginning to really like this girl.

Then, on a Saturday night in early March, four City seniors got into in a serious car crash. The Volkswagen bug, driven by Jimmy DeMars, struck a tree on McCallie Avenue near UTC. Jimmy was killed and the three passengers—Paul Carter, Amy Weaver, and Paula Pitt—wound up in serious condition at the hospital. The news spread quickly, as it was on the front page of the *Chattanooga Times* on Sunday morning.

Just a few days earlier, the school had been in jubilation over the results of the wrestling team, but on Monday morning, it was a solemn place. In general, teenagers have a hard time understanding what death means. Most think it's something that happens to old people or soldiers at war. It's not supposed to happen to classmates in high school. But when it does happen, especially to someone you know, death becomes real. As a kid, you begin to understand that life can be short and you're not invincible.

Jim DeMars was well-liked. He was a member of Hi-Y and played baseball. On the day of the funeral, school was let out at noon, so teachers and students could attend the service, held at Oak Wood Baptist Church. Virtually the whole student body attended. Arch, Gary Seepe, Mike O'Neil, and I rode together. We all wore coats and ties; most of the attending students were dressed in their Sunday best.

I'd never been to a funeral before. I'd watched funerals at Pleasant Garden, the cemetery in back of our house, from a distance, but this was very different. It was similar to going to church, but more somber. Most of the girls were crying and wiped their eyes with Kleenex. Even some of the tough boys had watery eyes.

The Baptist preacher stepped to the pulpit and started off the service by saying, "Jim was a fine young man. He was active in the church, the community, and his school. Sometimes we don't understand why people leave this earth before their time, but God has a plan for all of us and God had a plan for Jim." He continued with several verses of scripture, then asked the congregation to pray for Jim's family and concluded by assuring the gathering that we shouldn't worry about Jim, who was now with the Heavenly Father.

Others spoke during the service about Jim, but Coach Duke, who knew him well, described his short life best by saying, "More than any of the students I've seen, here was a boy who was in love with life."

The service ended with the singing of "Amazing Grace."

From the church, the funeral procession headed to the grave-side portion of the service, held at a cemetery just a mile away from the City campus.

It was a very sad event and one that we wouldn't forget for a long time. For the first time in our lives, we realized that the young were vulnerable and that life was unpredictable.

While the passengers survived, they did have to deal with fairly serious injuries. Their recovery certainly cut into them being able to enjoy the final month of their senior year. They missed out on lot. Amy was a popular calendar girl who couldn't walk in graduation due to her knee injury. Paul, captain of the baseball team and starting right-fielder, missed the remainder of the season. Paula was the editor of the *Dynamo* yearbook and couldn't attend the final review before it went to press.

But how would the school react to the tragedy going forward?

Chapter 21

Spring Break

A week after the DeMar wreck, spring break began. The time off helped us put the tragedy out of our minds. We had a week without school and when we returned, it would be time for football. Some kids went to the beach, some visited colleges, and some stayed home. Cindy went to visit her aunt in Orlando. Arch and I spent most of our time at Chickamauga Lake, where Arch's family had a boat and a place.

Their one-acre lot was in a development called Shady Grove. It was north of the Bass Bay Marina and just around the corner from where TVA was building the Sequoyah nuclear power plant. It was covered in pine trees, had a small camper trailer parked on it, and a floating dock accommodated a ski boat. There were a couple picnic tables, a fire pit, and an outhouse.

Arch was an accomplished slalom water skier. Of course, he'd grown up skiing, so it was almost second nature to him. He made skiing look easy and I felt like I could do it. At least I was ready to give it a try.

Most people learn on two skis, then work their way to one ski, the slalom. But Arch encouraged me to try one ski first. Hey, why not?

Although the weather was warming up and the lake water was still relatively cold, according to Arch it was warm enough to ski. So he gave me instructions on how, then handed me a slalom ski. I donned the ski vest and jumped in the water and man! Was it cold! It took me a few seconds to catch my breath. I was already freezing, but I was determined to do it. I knew that I had to get up; Arch wouldn't let me in the boat until I did.

I put my feet in the ski boots, found the rope, got into position as instructed, and yelled at Arch, "Hit it!"

He floored it and the boat lurched forward.

I went about 20 yards before falling off to the right.

Of course, he thought this was funny and called, "Try it again!"

I went through the whole process another time. I had the rope positioned and the ski up. I was crouched, arms stiff. I yelled, "Go!"

He hit the gas, I jerked out of the water, and to my surprise, as well as Arch's, I stayed up. There I was, gliding on top of the water. I was able to go around the whole cove without falling. Of course, I stayed right behind the boat and didn't try any tricky stuff. When I tired out, I let go of the rope, dropped into the water, and swam over to the boat as it approached.

Arch was amazed; he said he'd never seen anybody get up as quick as I had. So we spent the rest of spring break going to the lake and water skiing. It was a blast! I had a new passion.

It had been a fun week, but on Monday it was back to school—and the start of spring football practice. I was really looking forward to it. I was confident I could make the team and become a starter in the fall. In my previous spring practice at Castle Heights, I'd done well, making varsity as a sophomore as a result of my performance as a second-semester freshman. My road back to football started Monday and I was ready.

Chapter 22

Bad Break

The obvious talk around the school was about what went on during spring break. Cindy joined me for lunch in the Commons with one of her friends, Nancy Fryar. I'd seen Nancy around school, but hadn't met her. Cindy told me about her trip to Florida and Nancy kept asking me questions about my background, which was okay, but I was more interested in hearing what Cindy had to say.

There was a party Saturday night at Ray Gorrell's house. Marc was taking Gigi and wanted me to double-date with Cindy. My guess was that Cindy knew all along I'd ask her out. She just didn't know when. When I finally did, she said yes, so we made plans to go the party.

Finally! A date in my junior year, plus spring football was ready to start. We'd spend the next three weeks in pads, practicing. Almost 90 boys came out for the team—a huge turnout. The City football program had really gained in popularity, due to the success of the previous year. Coach Davis was building a program and guys wanted to be part of it.

The first day, equipment was issued. This time, rather than get what was left over, I actually received relatively new equipment. I even landed a locker in the varsity locker room. It was time to prove that I was a football player.

I was so excited to get on the field, I felt like running all the way—and we practiced on the lower field, probably 300 yards down at the bottom of the hill. It was called the lower field, but when you came back uphill after practice, it was called the

Cardiac Hill, because you sometimes felt like you were having a heart attack as you walked up the steep incline after a long practice. Still, I couldn't wait. I was completely confident that once I got on the field, I'd show the coaches what I could do and earn a starting position as an offensive and defensive back.

Spring practice could have been called "Test the Knees Practice." A bunch of guys had to sit out the previous season due to knee injuries. In those days, knee surgery required about a six-inch cut on the side of the knee, followed by about three months of immobilization and six to nine months of rehabilitation, but there were no rehab centers to speak of and physical therapists were few and far between. For the most part, the guys with knee injuries had to figure out rehab on their own or with the help of a coach. Arch, Lee Abelson, Tommy Richmond, Marvin Day, Jim Brown, David Soloff, and Shelton Goldblatt were all coming off some form of knee surgery.

We started practice with the usual calisthenics. Then we split up into groups of backs and linemen and ran through a set of drills, such as passing, tackling, and blocking. We spent the last hour running plays and scrimmaging.

At the beginning of the scrimmage, I was working with the offense at the right halfback position. We ran a variety of plays, mostly runs, but also a pass play or two. We'd run through about 10 plays and I'd gotten to run the ball some and block on the others. So far so good.

The next play was called and I was assigned to block the right defensive end. The ball was snapped, the end came rushing in, and I stepped up to block him. I positioned my forearms to deliver the blow to the onrusher. As I was moving my arms toward his body, he lowered his head and my left hand hit his face mask. I successfully made the block, but damn, the way I hit his face mask caused me a lot of pain. I wasn't going to let that stop me, of course; I'd waited over a year to get on the field with the varsity.

My hand continued to hurt during the remainder of practice and by the time we finished running wind sprints and walked up Cardiac Hill, it was pretty swollen. When I got home that night, I showed it to my father. He said, "I think it's broken."

Gee, that was great. Another setback to my football career. That night I put ice on it, took some aspirin, and hoped that it would clear up by morning.

When I woke up, my hand was about the size of a softball. I took another aspirin and went to school. During lunch, I showed Coach Davis my hand.

He said, "Yep, it looks like it's broken. Go see Dr. Dodds and he'll fix it for you."

Dr. Dodds was the team doctor. I went to his office. He took a couple of x-rays and sure enough, I'd broken the knuckle on my left ring finger. Dr. Dodds put my hand in a cast and said it would be six weeks before I could use it. That meant no contact. All I could do was run.

I viewed this as another crushing blow to my football career, because now I wouldn't get to participate in the remainder of spring football. I'd only have the summer to showcase my skills and earn a spot on the team. Surprisingly, Coach Davis was fairly optimistic and encouraging. He told me not to worry about it. During the remainder of spring, I could work out with the track team and do what I could with the football team.

Meanwhile, across town, Central High was also holding its first spring practice at the new location, but we heard that they didn't have the focus we did. We were already focused on them, whereas the Purple Pounders were still in a state of shock over the departure of Coach Etter. The assistant coaches were running spring practice with the emphasis on conditioning and drills. The players were more focused on who would be coaching them the following season than fine-tuning their offense. They were more or less just going through the motions, knowing that they'd have to prove themselves all over again when the new coach arrived in the summer. The most storied high-school football program in Chattanooga was like a ship without a rudder.

I became a spectator on the sidelines at football practice. It was tough not being on the field. Only being able to run wasn't much fun, but I got in shape.

Well, even if I did have a broken hand and was disappointed about my football status, I was looking forward to my first date with Cindy on Saturday night.

Chapter 23

The Date

Saturday night rolled around. I was picking up Cindy and meeting Marc and Gigi at Pizza Hut on Hixson Pike. Gigi and Cindy lived on opposite ends of town, so it made sense to meet, eat, and go to Ray's.

I drove my father's Ford Galaxy to pick her up. I knocked on the door and her dad answered. Inviting me in, he said, in a monotone, "So you're Buck."

I replied, "Yes sir."

He asked me what happened to my hand, so I told him the story. He introduced me to Cindy's mother and about that time, Cindy came into the room. We exchanged a few niceties with her parents, then left.

The four of us had a good time at dinner, mostly laughing about the daily events at City. Cindy had some funny stories and Gigi seemed to laugh at everything. She had one of those laughs that just made you laugh. We laughed so much that our sides hurt. After a couple pizzas and a pitcher or two of Coke, we headed to Ray's.

It was a small gathering of eight or so couples, including Ray, Arch, and Gary and their dates. Everyone there went to City High. Ray had made up some rum punch and Arch had made a trip to Granny's for beer. The stereo was cranked up and blasting music from the Jackson Five, Beatles, Four Tops, and Diana Ross. As the night went on, some couples left or went off to be by themselves. The party was beginning to quiet down.

Cindy and I walked out onto the front porch and sat down on the swing. We were having a friendly conversation and getting along rather well, so I went to put my arm around her and maybe steal a kiss. She sat on my left side and as I moved my arm around behind her, I accidentally hit her in the head with my cast and damn near knocked her out of the swing! We were both lucky I didn't knock her out cold. I told her I was sorry and she said, "That's okay, Buck. I've got a hard head, but I'm sure I'll have a knot on it tomorrow."

"I guess I'm not used to this ten-pound mallet on my hand."

"And I'm the one who's clumsy, while you're the graceful athlete."

We started laughing. Oh well, so much for that smooth move.

Cindy had to be in by 11:30, so when it was time to leave, I took her home.

As I walked her to the door, she asked, "Would you like to come in?"

I said, "Sure."

We walked into the kitchen and on the table was a photograph of me when I was about five year old. I was dressed in a white shirt and shorts and I was hugging a lady in a white dress. I recognized the picture, taken when I went to kindergarten at Brainerd Baptist Church, but I didn't recognize the lady. Lo and behold, it was Cindy's mother Catherine, who was my kindergarten teacher. Cindy and I hadn't put that together, but her mom certainly did! Talk about a weird coincidence. I wasn't sure whether it was a good sign or not. But then I figured it should be a good thing, since I was a sweet kid at that age.

As we were saying good night, I asked, "If I promise not to whack you in the head again, would you like to go out with me another time?"

I could see a little sparkle in her green eyes before she responded with a smile and an enthusiastic, "Yes!"

Chapter 24

Still on the Sidelines

Spring football rolled on and I continued to run and watch from the sidelines. Everyone who'd be playing in the fall, except the baseball players, was practicing. As you can imagine, there was a lot of competition, with 90 players trying out for the team. One of those players was Arch, who was mainly working out as a defensive back. But he wasn't getting along with Coach Davis. Arch was pissed, because Coach Davis wouldn't let him play much offense. Arch wanted to play halfback.

One day after practice, Arch went into Davis's office to talk to him about his status on the team. He asked the coach, "Why aren't I getting a shot at offense?"

Davis told him, "I want to see what other players can do."

"Why?" Arch asked.

"Well, since you're fifth string, I just don't see you playing much offense."

"Fifth string!" Arch exploded. "I've never been fifth-string anything!"

With that outburst, the meeting was over. Davis was right: Even with me being sidelined with a broken hand, the competition for running back was fierce. There were a lot of guys who had experience running the ball, but not as much when it came to defensive backs. If Arch wanted to play, it would be on defense. Even that wasn't a sure thing. He was competing against Denny Cornett for a cornerback spot. And Denny was a fairly athletic guy who also played basketball.

One thing about being on the sidelines watching practice

was I got a good idea who could play. I was impressed with the toughness of Pat Petty. Although Pat was small for a lineman, he made up for it being tough and quick. As a guard, he could pull when we ran the power sweeps. This was a real plus, especially when you had a fleet-footed back like Eddie Roberson running the ball. On defense, Pat played nose tackle and he could penetrate the backfield before the center was able to get out of his stance.

Eddie Roberson had played a lot the previous season. He was the son of a preacher and had grown up in North Chattanooga. His dad, Marshall Roberson, had been the pastor at North Chattanooga Church of God for many years; before that, he'd held preaching positions in Cleveland and Nashville. In the early fifties, he had even been the chaplain for death-row inmates in the Tennessee prison system. It was clear that Eddie was a gifted athlete. When we ran sprints, he was the only one on the team I couldn't beat.

There was no doubt that Bill Wilder would be the quarterback. He wasn't flashy, he didn't wow you with his throws or his runs, but he didn't make many mistakes and he had command of the huddle. He was a good leader and had the respect of the team.

When he showed up, Eddie Steakley was impressive as a receiver. But true to his erratic character, he continued to get into trouble at school. Spending his afternoons in detention hall caused him to miss practice. He even got suspended for a couple of days. When he put his mind to it, he was a force to be reckoned with on the football field. He was big and could catch a football. He didn't work hard, but he didn't have to; he had a lot of natural talent. You could tell that Steakley was one of Coach Davis's special projects. Davis worked to get him focused on football rather than trouble. He even put in a few plays just for Steakley, such as a quick jump pass, the quick slant, and a halfback pass.

The kicking game looked promising with John Cooper. He'd handled the kickoffs and extra points on varsity the year before. This year, it appeared he would handle all of the kicking duties, including punting.

On the line it looked like Lee Abelson and Tommy Richmond would anchor the left side. Pat Petty would join Joe Burns on the right. Joe got in a lot of playing time his junior year.

The offense was coming together.

On the defensive side of the ball, it wasn't as clear as to who would be playing. Davis put most of his focus on the offense in the spring. I guess he felt like this was the most difficult to sort out, since he had only a few starters returning from last year. Defensively, there were enough athletes that he could put together a pretty good group, even if some guys had to play both ways.

Overall, it looked like we would have a good team, but there was still a long way to go.

Of course, putting so many teenage boys together in a contact sport raised the inevitable personality clashes. One example surfaced with Eddie Roberson and Arnold Farmer, an end. Eddie was dating Ellen Jayne, but she seemed to be getting friendly with Arnold. Eddie thought Arnold was trying to move in on her. The two boys had words for a couple of days during school and at practice. Finally, things came to a head: Eddie challenged Arnold to a duel of fisticuffs. The plan was to meet after practice on the lower field.

After they got dressed, the boys and a few spectators went to the lower field. Eddie and Arnold walked out onto the field and started jawing at each other. Suddenly, Eddie reared back and hit Arnold square in the face, breaking his nose. Blood went everywhere as Arnold went down on the ground, hand to his face. The fight was over.

The next day, Eddie was called to the office to see Assistant Principal Jim Phifer, who gave him a handful of detentions for fighting on campus. Arnold didn't get any, since he didn't even throw a punch.

But Eddie's troubles from the altercation weren't over. When his dad, Reverend Roberson, found out about the fight, he made Eddie call Arnold's father and apologize. That was humiliating for the running back. Then, when Ellen found out about the fight, she was furious at Eddie. Eddie and Ellen's relationship ended and she and Arnold began dating.

Eddie learned an important lesson from this affair: It's better to be a lover than a fighter.

Spring practice was coming to an end, so football would be over for a while. There was a little more than month to go before we got out of school. After a year, I was no longer the new kid, of course, but my education about life at City High was far from over. I was about to find out where you shouldn't wear your high-school letter jacket.

Chapter 25

It's Time for a Cold One

President Nixon signed the Public Health Cigarette Smoking Act that banned cigarette advertising from being shown on TV. This was due, in part, to the fact that several years earlier, it had been determined that smoking causes cancer. Still, smoking was a well-accepted practice throughout the country. TV shows and movies portrayed smoking as the cool thing to do. People smoked freely in restaurants, stores, hotels, at sporting events, even on airplanes. The teachers could smoke at school. Coach Davis smoked in his office and on the field. Many other teachers smoked, either in the teacher's lounge or the classroom. Mrs. Wertheimer, the geometry teacher, took the cake.

In class as she wrote on the chalkboard, Mrs. Wertheimer's hand shook until she could light a cigarette. It was funny to see her write geometric formulas on the board with a cigarette hanging out of her mouth. She was a large-chested woman and at times it looked like the top of her chest was an ashtray. Although it was against the rules for students to smoke on campus, it wasn't uncommon to see them smoke around the school parking lot. Of course, Steakley preferred the school bathrooms.

I watched from the sidelines as we held our last scrimmage of the spring. It was a special scrimmage: the juniors against the sophomores in a regular game, only without the kicking. There was a lot of energy and some hard hitting on both sides, but as expected, the juniors had their way with the younger boys.

Near the end of the inter-squad game, a fight broke out after a running play between Steakley and John Gerber, a sophomore linebacker who weighed about 165 pounds. Apparently,

Eddie had been holding John on every play that was run on Eddie's side and John was tired of it. He started pushing the big end and it escalated into quite a fight before the coaches broke it up. But it continued in the locker room, where Steakley started picking at Gerber. John barked back and that led to them pushing each other around. Then Steakley sucker-punched John in the jaw. (As I got to know more about Eddie, I learned this was one of his favorite tricks. He hit you when you weren't expecting it.) John fell back about four feet and landed hard on the concrete floor. John jumped to his feet and went right after Steakley with fire in his eyes. It was another all-out fight like the one on the practice field, but this time there were no pads or helmets. Steakley's size was too much for Gerber, but John didn't quit until we pulled them apart. John looked like hell, his nose bloody and his right eye swollen shut. We kept them apart until they were dressed and left the locker room. The next day, Coach Davis had both of them in his office before practice and made them apologize to each other and the team.

The last day of practice, Coach Davis let the team go early after running through a few plays and, of course, ten wind sprints. The good news was the running was over with for a couple of months.

As we walked up Cardiac Hill, Pat suggested we go have a beer. He was planning to meet Marc at the Tempo Tap Room, a small building on Cherokee Boulevard across the street from the Krystal. Now, I wasn't sure how we were going to get a beer at the Tempo, but if Pat said we could, it was okay with me.

We parked down the street and walked toward the bar. I was wearing a Tennessee athletic jacket and Pat was wearing his City High letter jacket. It was maroon and trimmed in white with a large white "C" on the left-front panel. Pat had earned two letters this year, one in football and the other in wrestling.

He loved that jacket and wore it everywhere.

As we walked into the tavern, Marc was already seated at the bar drinking a beer. The bartender eyed Pat with a serious look on his face. I thought for sure we were in trouble. I didn't know if he was going to call the cops or just throw us out. He walked over to edge of the bar where we were standing, glared at Pat, and said, "I've told you before not to wear your high-school jacket in the bar."

Pat apologized, took off his jacket, and folded it up. I had to smile over the situation: Apparently, it was okay to service underage drinkers, as long they didn't advertise the fact by wearing a high-school jacket.

The bartender served us a couple draft beers without asking for ID or anything else. They were ice cold and cost only a quarter apiece. Now we were celebrating the end of spring football in style at the Tempo Tap Room. I was learning that as long as you went to a North Chattanooga bar with a local boy who knew the owner, you could get served without question. I was getting quite an education at Chattanooga High School.

After a couple of beers, Marc and I went over to pick up Arch. The three of us were going up the mountain to drop by a slumber party for a while. Arch wanted to drive, but instead of heading to Frazier Avenue, the normal way to Signal Mountain, he went the other direction.

I asked him, "Where are you going?"

He said, "To Gorrell's. I've got some business to take care of before we head up the mountain."

It was a short drive to Ray's house. We pulled up and saw Ray's old gray Rambler sitting out front, so Ray was probably home.

Arch said, "Buck, open the glove compartment and hand me the gun."

I gave him a puzzled look. "What are you going to do with the gun?"

He said, "Nothing much. I'm just fixing to scare Gorrell a little bit, that's all."

I handed him the gun, he rolled down his window, and before I knew it, he fired four bullets into the old Rambler, breaking out the back windows. The car was only about 20 feet from the house, so there was a good chance a round hit that. Arch didn't wait around to find out. He handed me the gun, told me to put it back in the glove compartment, hit the gas, and got out of there in a hurry.

Marc and I were stunned.

I yelled, "What the hell did you do that for? You could have killed someone!"

Arch said, "I'm just pissed off at Ray," and he went to explain that Ray had been seeing a girl Arch had also been going out with.

Marc and I looked at each other with raised eyebrows. That didn't seem like a reason to shoot up someone's car. It was a quite ride up the mountain that night. Marc and I didn't know what to say. We just hoped that Arch never got really pissed off at us!

That was a hell of a way to end spring football. I would check the paper in the morning to see if there was a reported homicide in North Chattanooga.

Chapter 26

Let's Dance

There was nothing in the paper Saturday morning about the drive-by shooting at Gorrell's house. And on Monday after homeroom I saw Ray, so fortunately Arch hadn't killed him Friday night. Word gets around high school in a hurry, because no one can keep a secret. So Ray knew that Arch had been the triggerman on his car, but he didn't say anything to him about it. At the end of the week, Arch went over to Ray's to apologize and offer to pay for the repairs.

Ray told Arch, "Hell, there's no reason to get pissed off about a girl. I just went out with her one time. You and I have been friends too long to let some girl get between us. Next time, just tell me you're pissed off rather than shooting up my damn car!"

By now, I was pretty used to being in a cast. My only difficulties were with Mrs. Griffith, my typing teacher. Up until breaking my hand, I was one of the better typists in the class. This was because one of E. Blaine's summer programs for me was typing. When I wasn't moving bricks around the backyard, he assigned me typing lessons. So over the previous four summers, I'd learned how to type on an old Royal manual typewriter. But it took three full weeks of sitting in class, unable to complete the speed and accuracy drills and tests for two hands that Mrs. Griffith expected me to do with one, before she finally relented. She told me that if I just attended class for the rest of the semester, she'd give me a "B." Though I'd been an "A" typing student previously, I thought that was a good compromise. It was certainly better than an incomplete and having to retake the class in the summer or the fall.

The national news reported that Paul McCartney was leaving the Beatles. This came as quite a shock; the group that had changed the music world forever was splitting up. The Spring Fling dance was coming up and I was sure the band would still play plenty of our favorite Beatles songs.

Cindy was on the committee to set up the Spring Fling, held in April. The committee had to plan the dance, hire the band, make the posters and signs, blow up balloons, and sell the tickets. One day at lunch, she asked if I'd go with her to the dance. Of course, I said, "Yes," and we agreed to make a night of it.

On the night of the Spring Fling, I picked Cindy up. I was wearing a blue blazer, a blue oxford-cloth button-down-collar shirt with a tie and gray slacks. Cindy was dressed in a pink pantsuit. She looked great, it was my first dance at City, and I was excited to be going with this cute blond! We didn't stop talking all the way to the restaurant. We met Marc and Gigi, Tommy Richmond and Patty Varnell, and Sally Fuston and Freddy White at the Town and Country. Sally was good friends with Cindy and Gigi. Freddy went to McCallie, where he played football and wrestled. His brother Petey was a senior at City. Freddy had met Sally at a City party he'd gone to with his brother.

The Town & Country, by a high-school student's standard, was a fancy restaurant. We boys were really watching what we ordered because of the expense, so we ate the cheapest thing on the menu: cheeseburgers. The girls got what they wanted. The conversation centered on the latest gossip, such as who was dating and who was breaking up, who was failing which class, and who'd been caught drinking. Of course, Tommy and I talked about football.

After dinner, we headed to the school, but along the way, we took a quick detour by the Krystal to get a couple of Cokes to go. In the school parking lot, Marc pulled out a bottle of Bacardi from the glove compartment, which we mixed with the Cokes. After finishing our drinks, we headed to the Commons.

A faculty member was posted at the entrance to the dance to check the students as they came in. Although we'd had only one drink, we didn't want to get caught with liquor on our breath. So the plan was to enter through the door where the Spanish teacher, Don Smith, was stationed. We could count on Smith to look the other way for those who entered a little tipsy; he also ignored the drinking going on during the dance. There was a good chance that Miss Prior would be standing guard at the main door. If she smelled liquor on your breath, she'd grab you by the ear and drag you to the principal's office. Smith's door was the way!

Mr. Smith—or Don Juan as he was sometimes called—was a "cool" teacher. He was always friendly with the students, especially the girls, thus the nickname. He wore glasses and his hair was slicked back. He was always dressed well and he drove a red Chevrolet Impala convertible. Everyone wanted to be in his class because of his fairly lenient grading system. It was rumored that the only way Spook McKelvy got a passing grade in Mr. Smith's first-semester Spanish I class was by bribing Don Juan with a sleeve of golf balls. I couldn't help wondering that if someone gave him four sleeves and didn't even show up for class, would Smith give out an "A"?

By the time we got in, the dance was in full swing. The Commons, which also served as the dance hall, was highly decorated and Cindy pointed out her handiwork as we walked around the edge of the dance floor. The band was rocking out at a deafening level. They played the popular rock 'n' roll tunes of the day. The music by the Beatles, Elton John, Four Tops, Doors, the Supremes, Otis Redding, Stevie Wonder, Michael

Jackson, and others rang out through the venue. Frankly, the band was pretty doggone good.

When we first arrived, not many people were dancing, mostly hanging out around the perimeter, watching the few that were actually out on the dance floor. There was a refreshment area where punch and cookies were served. A rumor was going around that one of the seniors had spiked the punch, but after three glasses, I determined that wasn't true. As the night went on, more kids began to dance. Some were twisting or shagging, while others were moving around like their hair was on fire. Slow songs were the most popular and got a lot dancers on the floor. Of course, it drove Ms. Prior crazy as she tried to police the couples and make sure there was no inappropriate touching or rubbing going on. If she saw anything she didn't approve of, she tapped the boy on the shoulder, wagging her figure at him and shaking her head: "No!" Much to my surprise, I found myself out on the floor, dancing with Cindy and finding out that I liked it. The last dance I'd been to was my sophomore year at the military school. We danced until the band's last song.

There was an after-dance party at Ray's, but it was already late, so we had to go home. We both had curfews. We arrived at Cindy's before the imposed time, so she asked me in and we sat down on the couch in the den.

We talked while we watched TV. After about ten minutes, her Siamese cat Stella strolled into the room. Stella looked at me like, "Who are you and what are you doing here?" First, she sashayed over and sniffed my leg. Then she turned around, walked over, and in one graceful leap, jumped on top of the TV. She curled up in a ball with her head facing the wall and her tail hanging down over the screen. The tail was positioned right in the center of the screen. Though the cat appeared to be asleep, about every 30 seconds she moved her tail from left to right in a pattern similar to the windshield wipers on a car. This made it difficult to concentrate on "The Johnny Carson Show." After about 30 minutes of watching the cat's tail go back and forth, I headed for home.

On the way home, I tried to figure out what message Stella the cat was trying to send me with her twitching tail. Maybe she was the Ms. Prior of the Frazier household.

I'd had a great time at the dance and hoped Cindy did too. I liked being with her, but I wasn't sure where our relationship was going. I'd never had a steady girlfriend before and I could see the pluses and the minuses of it. If you had a girlfriend, you always had someone to talk to, go to the movies with, or go on dates with other couples. But on the down side, I could see that some of my fun would be sacrificed, like hanging out with the guys, going to the lake whenever I wanted to, or chasing other girls. I guessed time would tell.

Chapter 27

The Squeeze Play

The national news of the week concerned Apollo 13. It was scheduled to be the third trip to the moon, but an oxygen tank exploded two days into the mission, causing a loss of cabin heat, a shortage of potable water, and buildup of carbon dioxide in the cabin, any one of which put the astronauts in grave danger. Not only did they have to scrap the moon landing, but there was a chance that they wouldn't return to Earth. Fortunately, the astronauts, led by Captain Jim Lovell and with the help of the Houston Space Center, were able to make the necessary repairs. After seven tense days in space, the crippled spaceship splashed down safely in the South Pacific near Samoa.

The baseball season was now in full swing. We all expected the Dynamo boys to do quite well. The head coach was Jimmy Duke. He was also the boys' assistant basketball coach. Coach Duke liked athletes, but didn't have much time for anyone else. Once he found out I played football, he always spoke to me in the halls. He sometimes joked around with the ballplayers by showing off his boxing moves and quick hands. Apparently, he'd been quite a boxer in his younger days in the Golden Gloves. Coaching was his passion and there was no joking around when it came to baseball. On the ball field, he was all business.

Duke pushed his teams to excel. They played ball in the spring and summer; winters, they worked out inside. The team was led by seniors Bob Corker, Fred Hilliard, Charlie Ryder, and Bobby Leffew. Bobby, along with Foster Yates and Randy S. Gray, did most of the pitching. Kenny Smith provided speed and played in the outfield. The team played its home games at

Engle Stadium. It was built in 1930 and had been the home of the Chattanooga Lookouts of the Southern League for almost 40 years. Unfortunately, the Lookouts last played there in 1965 and since then, only high school, college, and amateur teams played at the grand old stadium.

I always enjoyed going to baseball games and I regretted that I didn't play baseball in high school. It was my first love and I was probably better at baseball than I was at football. I'd played up until the tenth grade and after that, I focused on football. My father had taken me to a lot of Lookout games. If they were in town, we might attend a couple times a week; he really liked the Sunday double headers—two games for the price of one. The only down side was when you went to a game with E., you got there for the first pitch and didn't leave until the last, even if it was a lopsided score. He wanted to make sure he got his money's worth. It was a lot fun watching the game and my dad always bought me a Coke and a pack of baseball cards.

So going to City High games at Engle Stadium was a real treat for me, because it brought back fond memories of the old ball park. City was playing Brainerd for the second time in two weeks. It was the final game of the regular season; a win would clinch the district title for the maroon and white. I got to the game early and watched the Dynamos take the field. It was impressive. Coach Duke ran the infield drills like a major-league team. He was exceptional with a fungo bat. He could place the ball virtually anywhere he wanted to, whether it was on the ground or high in the air.

As Kenny Smith stood in the outfield catching fly balls, I knew he had something on his mind other than the game. This was the day when he hoped to finally get a date with Sammye Smith. A good-looking girl who always dressed nicely, Sammye had been dating a boy from Baylor for eight or nine months.

During the previous fall, the Baylor boy had sponsored her and she'd been selected as the 1969 Baylor Homecoming Queen. Kenny had been trying to get a date with her for the past two months. They were in the same homeroom, so he had the opportunity to talk to Sammye daily. She seemed interested in him, but wouldn't commit to a date, telling him she'd go out with him "sometime." Kenny had grown tired of waiting, so he gave her an ultimatum: If she didn't come to the Brainerd game, he'd give up on her and look for someone else. There was, however, a fly in the ointment; the night of the Brainerd game, Sammye was supposed to go to the Dionne Warwick concert with her Baylor boyfriend.

After the infield drills, the team headed to the dugout. As Kenny jogged off the field, he looked up in the stands and there, behind the dugout, was Sammye sitting next to Cindy.

Engle Stadium was considered our home field, so it was City's job to take care of the field, collect the tickets, manage the concession stand, run the scoreboard, and retrieve foul balls. The old stadium's roof covered about two-thirds of the stadium's seats. On top of the roof was the press box. During games, it wasn't uncommon for 10 or 12 foul balls to land on the roof. So Coach Duke arranged for someone to be stationed there to retrieve them. The deal was if you spent one game on the roof, you worked off three detentions. It was easy duty; the roof was flat and had a fence all the way around the edge, so you didn't have to worry about falling off while retrieving balls. It was also a great place to watch the games. Spook and Steakley were regulars for roof duty.

The game started out badly for the Dynamos. Randy S. Gray gave up five runs in the top of the first inning. He'd only recorded two outs when Duke replaced him with senior Bobby Leffew. Bobby stopped the bleeding, got the last out of the inning, and held them in check until he ran out of gas in the fifth when he gave up one run. Then Foster Yates came in and got the final two outs. City fought its way back to tie the game at six. In the top of the seventh, Foster once again held Brainerd scoreless. Tennessee high-school games go seven innings unless there's a tie; then the teams go into extra innings. Since we were the home team, we'd get a chance to win the game in the bottom of the seventh.

Charlie Ryder led off with a double to left center. He advanced to third on a sacrifice fly. Now Charlie stood at third base with one out. Foster Yates was due up to bat. Foster was no Mickey Mantle, and I had no doubt that Duke considered sending in a pinch hitter. But the bull pen was thin and with the chance that the game could go into extra innings, he let Yates hit for himself.

Foster took a look down at Coach Duke at third base for the sign. The batter's options were to bunt, hit, or take the pitch (and not swing). Coach Duke could flash signs like a pro, touching his belt, letters, face, ears, hat, or arms. This time Coach Duke slowly walked to the back of the third-base coaching box without giving any kind of a sign. Everyone in the Dynamo dugout and half of us in the stands knew that this "no-sign" stroll called for the suicide squeeze.

Coach Duke loved to call the squeeze play when there was a runner on third. The batter's job was to bunt the ball into fair territory. The base runner started toward home plate as the pitcher released the ball. It was called a "suicide" squeeze, because if the batter didn't connect on the bunt, all the catcher had to do was take the pitch and tag out the runner coming home. Getting tagged out at home plate is baseball's version of a self-inflicted shot to the head. On the other side, if the play is executed properly, it's almost impossible to defend.

Davis May, the Brainerd pitcher, wound up and fired off the pitch. Charlie Ryder broke for the plate, but Foster made no attempt to bunt the ball. He simply watched it go by. The umpire called it a strike. The catcher bobbled the ball as Charlie put on the breaks and hustled back to third without a throw.

Coach Duke walked around in circles for a minute, then went back to the front of the box and stared at Foster.

Unfazed, Foster looked back for the sign.

Coach Duke gave the no-sign again.

Okay, now both teams and everyone in the stands knew what was coming. Davis May stretched and delivered the ball. Once again, Charlie broke for home and once again Foster kept the wooden bat on his shoulder. The umpire signaled ball. The catcher took the ball and threw down to third. Once again, Charlie put on the brakes and scampered back to the base. The throw from the catcher was high and Charlie dove head first into the bag just under the tag by the third baseman.

Coach Duke took his hat off, looked at the scoreboard, and walked around in circles. Everyone in or watching the game— except Foster, of course—could see that he was so mad, he could chew nails. He stared at Foster, red-faced. And again, he retreated to the back of the coaching box. I couldn't believe he was calling for the squeeze a third time!

May went into his stretch, looked back at Charlie at third, then delivered the ball toward the plate. Charlie broke for home. The pitch, a curveball, bounced in the dirt in front of the plate and got by the catcher. Foster once again made no effort to bunt, but the catcher chased the ball to the backstop. Charlie slid over home plate and scored the winning run. City had just won the District Championship, seven to six.

Foster and all the players were jumping for joy in celebrating the victory. Coach Duke, however, was still standing in the coach's box with his hands on his hips, staring at the scoreboard. As the boys headed toward the dugout, the coach turned around and made a beeline straight toward Foster.

Foster had pitched great and won the game. Unbeknownst to Yates, though, Coach Duke was just steps away. He pushed his way through the celebrating players and grabbed Foster. The veins in the coach's neck were popping out and his face was bright red. He started yelling at Foster. "How in the hell can you miss not one, not two, but *three* suicides-squeeze signs?"

Foster's jubilation for pitching a great game was short-lived, especially when the former boxer pushed him back, knocking over the water cooler, penning him up against the wall, and still yelling about the missed signs. Some of Foster's teammates thought Duke might actually kill him with some of those Golden Glove boxing moves. Fortunately for both of them, the coach didn't hit him. Foster lived to pitch another day, but never missed a sign again!

Though the team had won the championship game, Kenny Smith still had other things on his mind: He was taking Sammye out to dinner. Cindy went along, since she was spending the night with Sammye. After dinner, Cindy drove as Sammye and Kenny sat in the back seat and got to know each other better. It was a successful first date, but was it good enough for Sammye to break up with her boyfriend?

Chapter 28

The English Scholar

The next Saturday, we were scheduled to take the ACT College Board entrance test at City's library.

There were two entrance tests, the ACT and SAT. I was told most colleges in the South favored the ACT. Since I hated taking these standardized tests, I'd only take one, so I picked the ACT. It took the entire morning and after the test, I felt like I'd been through the ringer.

About a month later, we got the results back. I'd scored just high enough to get into the state universities, which was good enough for me. On the other hand, Cindy, Mike O'Neil, and Eddie Francisco had recorded almost the maximum score. Gee, with those scores, they might have to consider going to an Ivy League school. I was glad I didn't have that problem.

We'd just beaten Brainerd in baseball, but the big story at Brainerd was that racial tensions were heating up again. It'd started the previous October, when black students protested the use of Confederate symbols to identify the school; the teams were called the Rebels, the Confederate flag was the school icon, and the fight song was "Dixie." The week-long city-wide curfew obviously hadn't solved this problem.

Brainerd had about 1,400 students and of that, 180 of them were black. They'd been going there for only a couple of years and the school was slow to include them in the social scene. The October protesting went on for a couple days, but then things settled back to normal. It had been fairly quiet, but now, fights between whites and blacks were breaking out in the halls, bathrooms, and cafeteria. The police were called in to patrol during school hours. After-school activities were cancelled. Even the annual Spring Art Festival was cancelled.

The presence of the police didn't curtail the violence. A group of black boys caught two white boys in a bathroom and beat them so badly they had to be taken to a local hospital. One day after school, as black students boarded a school bus, they were attacked by a number of white students. School officials broke up the disturbance, but in retaliation, the white students sat down in front of the bus to prevent it from leaving the campus. Police arrived, dispersed the crowd, and escorted the bus off the school property.

Racial tensions escalated to the point where Brainerd had to be closed on and off for two weeks. Civic clubs, politicians, church leader, parents, and school-board officials were involved in resolving the issue. One of the headlines in the *News Free Press* read, "Negros Meet Mayor on Brainerd." Finally, with only a few weeks remaining in the school year, things settled down and school got back to normal. Fortunately, again, City High didn't have such a problem; for some reason, blacks were welcome there.

Kenny Smith had finished up a good year on the basketball court and was playing well on the baseball diamond. But school was just a way for Kenny to get to play sports. Kenny considered his priorities to be sports first, girls second, and school third. He was an okay student, but he hated English and it didn't take much of an excuse for him to skip the class. Warned several times by his basketball coach, Jim Phifer, not to cut English class, Kenny assured the coach that he wouldn't do it anymore, but he did. I guess Kenny didn't realize that Coach Phifer was also the assistant principal. Then one day in April, an announcement came over the intercom for Kenny to report to the principal's office.

Kenny thought that Phifer wanted to talk to him about something related to basketball. But as he turned the corner into the coach's office, he saw a boot in the corner of the doorway. Kenny's heart dropped; the boot was his father's.

The last person Kenny expected to see in the office was his father. Kenny was speechless. He could only muster a soft, "Hey," to his dad. His father was a tough man. He'd boxed in high school and well into his 20s. He'd worked his way up the ranks at the local power company. He was a man of few words. His look cut right through Kenny and said, "If I have to come up here again for any reason other than to watch you play ball, you won't have to worry about missing class anymore, because I'm going to kill you."

After that short but clear message, Mr. Smith got up and left Kenny sitting there with the two coaches. The young Smith, white-faced and in a state of shock, turned to Coach Phifer and said, "Coach, I promise I won't cut any more English classes this year."

The coach turned to him and said, "You're right. I know you won't miss any more English, because I'm going to be your English teacher for the remainder of the year."

Coach Phifer, who'd taught English teacher earlier in his career, became Kenny's personal English teacher. From that point on, when it came time for English class, Kenny reported to Coach Phifer's office. During the next several weeks, Kenny did more English homework than he had the previous two years.

Fortunately for Kenny, there was only a month left in the school year.

Myself, I was in pretty good shape with my grades. I wouldn't make honor roll, but it looked like the worst I'd do was a "C" or two.

Since this was my first year at City, I didn't really know

what to expect the last month of the school year, but if it was anything like the last seven months, I knew it would be memorable.

Chapter 29

The Last Month of School

One of the history teachers, Miss Ward, was fairly young with red hair. She'd recently written an article about Dr. Jim Henry that appeared in the *Chattanooga News Free Press* in which she praised him for his service to public education in Chattanooga. The article went on to talk about Henry's dedication to City High School and what a great guy he was to work with.

A few days after the article appeared, Spook walked into Miss Ward's class and commented, "I read your article in the paper about Dr. Henry. It was real good. You must be running for teacher of the year."

She picked up a history book and threw it at him. Luckily for Spook, she missed.

With only one month of the semester left, most students were focused on anything but school. The seniors couldn't wait until they got to college in the fall. There were end-of-the-year celebrations, slumber parties, and trips out of town. Now that it was getting warm, any chance I got, I went to the lake. My cast was off my hand. I could use it, but I had difficulty bending my broken finger. Still, I could hold a ski rope. I planned to do as much water-skiing as I could between then and summer football practice.

One night, the national news led off with a shocking story. Walter Cronkite reported that four students at Kent State University in Ohio had been killed by the Ohio National Guard. Nine other students had been wounded and were taken to the hospital. The National Guard had been called in to put down a protest over the escalation of the Vietnam War into Cambodia that was on the verge of turning into a riot. The Kent State incident caused a ripple effect across the country, as student protests erupted on a number of college campuses. Over the next several days, more than 80 campuses across the country were closed due to these war-protest rallies. Fortunately in southeastern Tennessee, we avoided any protesting.

There had been many protests about the war over the past years, but the Kent State shootings forced most Americans to ask the question, "What is the purpose of the war?" At age 17, I considered myself a conservative. I was a "short-hair" guy and if I got called to go to Vietnam, I'd go. Up until Kent State, I viewed the protest as just a bunch of dope-smoking hippies causing trouble. Well, my opinion didn't change much, but it did cause me to think more about it. After all, Kent State wasn't California, the epicenter of the anti-establishment movement. It was in Middle America.

The United States had been involved in this war for over 10 years. The politicians viewed it as a necessary step to prevent the spread of communism in the Far East. It wasn't a conventional war as compared to the World Wars of the century. In those wars, when the U.S. got involved, the goal was simple: win the war. In World War II we defeated Germany and Japan in four years. How come we couldn't win a war against a bunch of rice farmers in ten years? Well, technically, it was a policing action, not a war. While the politicians and generals haggled over strategy goals, American boys were dying every day.

The popularity of military high schools had grown after War World II, but was now declining, mainly due to the perception of the military activity in Vietnam. Arch, who wasn't happy about the way spring football had gone, feeling that Coach Davis hadn't given him a fair break, told me he was thinking about transferring schools and was looking at going to Columbia Military Academy (CMA) in Columbia, Tennessee. CMA was in the same conference as Castle Heights. I'd played against them the year before. He could transfer there and still get to play his senior year, because their Mid-South Conference didn't have a sit-out rule.

Arch tried to talk me into going to school there with him and I told him, "No thanks!" I'd had my fill of military schools.

That night, we must have spent about three hours talking about military schools. By the end of the discussion, I thought I'd talked him into staying at City.

It was Saturday. I'd originally planned to go out with Cindy that night, but some of the guys wanted me to go to the Civitans initiation party at the lake, spend the night there, and ski the next day. I called Cindy to cancel the date. I could tell that she wasn't happy. I told her that I'd come to see her Sunday afternoon when I got back from the lake. She said, "Okay."

The initiation party was the rite of passage to full membership for sophomores, who were considered just pledges. Generally speaking, the initiation was just a reason to have a year-end party and raise a little hell by hazing the young members. I wasn't an official Civitan, but because of my friendship with members like Arch, Marc, and some of the football players, I was considered an honorary member. This meant that I was a member who hadn't gone through initiation.

The event was held at Peaky's Point on the lake about a mile south of Bass Bay, an isolated camping spot covered in pine trees. It was a perfect place for high-school kids to have a wild unsupervised party. There was a keg of beer and plenty of whiskey to go around.

Most of the boys had planned to spend the night in tents or in cars at the Point; however, Arch, Marc, David Soloff, and I were staying in Arch's trailer at his lake property.

I rode to the event with Soloff. David was a member of Hi Y. But he hung around with more Civitans than Hi Y boys. Most of the Civitans liked him, so it was okay for him to be there. David drove a brown and white '64 Buick, which at one time had been his father's business car. David wasn't the most prompt person, so when we arrived, the initiation was well underway.

We drove down the dirt road until we reached the camping area. He pulled the car over on the side of the dirt road and hastily parked between a couple trees. We jumped out of the car and headed off to watch the festivities.

The initiation process included beer chugging, running naked through an obstacle course, a question-and-answer session, and the stroke of approval. The Q&As consisted of an elder member asking random question; if the pledge didn't get the answer right, he was required to take a shot of whiskey. The final step to be fully vested in the club was the stroke of approval, which consisted of 10 licks on the bare ass with the "official" Civitans paddle.

After a couple of hours of watching the abuse of the young sophomores, David and I were ready to go. I told Arch we'd meet him there and we walked back to Soloff's car.

As we approached the car, I noticed that it was sitting in the middle off four pine trees we hadn't seemed to notice when David parked a few hours earlier. I didn't know how he got it parked in there in the first place, but the bigger question was how in the world would he get it out? David got behind the wheel and tried to maneuver the car between the trees, but the more we tried, the worse it got. After about 30 minutes, we came to the conclusion that we couldn't get the car out. In all likelihood, one of the four trees would have to be cut down in order to move the car.

David was a carefree guy and the stuck car didn't really seem to bother him. He just said, "Hey, I'll deal with it later." By now, Arch was ready to go, so we loaded up in Arch's car and headed up to his lot.

The next day, we cooked breakfast over the campfire, then headed out on the boat for a day of skiing. We ran out of gas and beer around the same time, so we went to Bass Bay Marina. Mr. Beard was the dock man who gassed up the boats and sold snacks and beer. Mr. Beard had a tendency to drink on the job and as the day went on, he forgot to check IDs. It was Sunday and in Tennessee, it was illegal to sell beer on Sundays due to the blue laws prevalent throughout the South. This didn't prevent Mr. Beard from selling us enough beer to get us through the day. My guess is he didn't really know what day it was.

We skied all day and it was almost seven o'clock by the time I got home. I knew Cindy would be pissed, so I convinced myself that it was too late call and I'd apologize to her tomorrow.

The next morning at school, I went to see Cindy where we normally met in front of her locker between second and third periods. As I approached her, she said, "I don't even want to talk to you."

I said, "I'm really sorry, Cindy."

She turned around and walked away without saying a word.

I didn't blame her, of course. I'd backed out on our Saturday night date and stood her up on Sunday. I guessed that was the end of that.

The next day, Soloff's dad sent David and a wrecker to Peaky's to get the Buick. The wrecker driver couldn't figure out how he parked the car inside the trees.

He told David he must have dropped it in by helicopter, because it was impossible for him to drive into that position.

They determined the easiest way to get the car out was to cut down the tree in back, which would allow more room to hook up the wrecker. So they cut down the 30-foot pine tree, hooked up the brown Buick to the wrecker, and pulled it free.

Chapter 30

The Drive-In

The next weekend, the Tri Hi Y girls had a slumber party at Michelle Medford's house on Signal Mountain. Sammye, Cindy, and Sheron Bunch would be heading up there. The Tri Hi Y girls had recently had their initiation party, but it was much tamer than the Civitans'. Blindfolding the new members and making them eat unrecognizable foods was about a daring as it got.

Michelle was a cheerleader and her family had recently moved into a large new house that sat on the brow of the mountain and overlooked the eastern part of Hamilton County. It had a playroom built just for kids, with a big TV, built-in stereo, and pool table. Right off the driveway, it was a great place for parties.

The room's ceiling had a smooth white-plaster finish. Michelle's mom wanted to start a tradition that anyone who came to a party for the first time signed their name, along with the date, on the ceiling in black magic marker. There were only a few names on the ceiling when Cindy, Sammye, and rest of the girls arrived, so they got the prime spots to apply autographs.

Michelle's parents weren't home when the girls got there. They went to the playroom, put some records on the stereo, and ate frozen pizza. Then, the plan was to go to the drive-in movies.

Drive-ins generally ran second-rate or older movies. They had a lot of double features and you could bet that at least one of the features would be either an Elvis or a monster movie. You really didn't go to the drive-in to see a movie. You went to hang out with friends or to take a date (you could always tell these cars; their windows were fogged up). The drive-ins were also really inexpensive. It cost a dollar a person to get in.

Sometimes, high-school kids didn't even have a dollar. In that case, as many kids who could fit hid in the trunk.

Now, there was a method to trunk smuggling. You didn't load up in the trunk until you got near the drive-in. Within a mile or so of the drive-in, the car pulled over at a gas station or parking lot, where the kids hopped in the trunk. After the car passed through the pay booth, the car headed to the far side of the parking area and the stowaways emerged.

With eight girls going to the drive-in, if they stuffed four girls in the trunks of the two cars, they'd have enough money for admission and refreshments for all eight. The only problem with this was Sammye's car, a Mustang, had a very small trunk. It was doubtful one girl could get in there, much less two. To see if they could fit two in the small compartment, they tested it in Michelle's driveway. Cindy and Sammye were selected for the Mustang test, because they were the smallest of the group. The two girls folded up and it looked like it would work. They just needed to shut the trunk lid to make sure. They shut the trunk and sure enough, they fit. Great! Now they could head to the drive-in.

That was when Sammye realized that she had the Mustang's keys in her pocket. What were they going to do now?

After about three minutes in the trunk, Cindy started panicking. "I can't breathe! I can't breathe!"

Sammye replied laughingly, "Oh yeah you can. There's plenty of air!"

The other girls tried to gain access from the back seat, but a solid piece of heavy plastic blocked it from the trunk.

About this time, Marvin Day rode up on his blue Honda 450 motorcycle. Marvin was staying with the Medfords for the time being, due to some family issues. As he dismounted his 450, the girls rushed over, explained the situation, and asked him to help get Cindy and Sammye out of the trunk. Marvin broke out laughing; he laughed so hard his sides hurt.

After he got himself under control, they surveyed the situation and it appeared that if they pried up the corner edge of the trunk lid, they could get a big enough opening to slide a key out.

The next trick was to get the key out of Sammye's pocket and to the corner of the trunk. Somehow the two girls managed to retrieve the keys. Then Sammye took her shoe off, reached down, put the key between her toes, and moved it toward the opening at the edge of the trunk. While Marvin bent the corner of the trunk up, Sheron got a coat hanger, stuck the curved end through the opening, and after tickling the bottom of Sammye's foot a couple of times, she hooked the key and pulled it out through the small opening. Now they would be free at last!

As the truck lid opened, all the girls burst out laughing so hard that tears rolled down their cheeks. After the trunk test, they headed off to the drive-in, but they paid admission for all the girls and did without Cokes and popcorn.

After the movie, the girls all went back to Michelle's house. There weren't enough beds to go around, so some of the girls slept on the floor in sleeping bags. Because of their ordeal, Cindy and Sammye were given a choice sleeping spot: They got to sleep in the huge walk-in closet, which could have slept several girls. It was so big it had a low window where you could look out into the valley below.

The Junior-Senior Prom was coming up. The Monday after the trunk incident, I asked Cindy if she wanted to go. She told me that she already had a date and was going with one of her old boyfriends, Tommy Fethe, who was a senior. I guessed I'd be going to the lake that night.

Chapter 31

The Class of 1970

In Knoxville, Tennessee, President Nixon and evangelist Billy Graham addressed a crowd of 70,000 at University of Tennessee's Neyland Stadium. The president urged turning to God as an answer to the recent unrest in the country. Billy Graham delivered the message. My guess was, this was one way the government tried to ease the pain from the recent protests and violence on college campuses. The Bible belt, of which Tennessee is part, was a good way to get positive support.

With the prom behind us, all that was left were finals and graduation. Our spring sports teams had done okay. The baseball team had won the district, but lost in the first round of the playoffs to Riverside. The all-black school's pitcher threw so slowly that he couldn't break a window. After seeing fastballs most of the year, the City hitter's couldn't adjust their timing at the plate to the slow speed. They got beat in the low-scoring affair.

The golf team was perfect, with only a tie to Central during the regular season. Then to cap things off, Coy Mabry and Mike Nelms placed first and second in the City Prep Tournament.

Brainerd ran away with the track meet, winning the district by over 21 points. They went on to win the state title. The bright spots for the Dynamos were Eddie Roberson placing second in the 100- and 200-yard dashes, while Joe Burns placed second in the shot put.

When it came to our old rival Central, we'd beaten them in all the sports in the second half of the year. We only needed to win in football to complete the domination for the entire year.

The pressure to end the 30-year football drought was mounting.

City's team calendar concluded with the Annual Sports Banquet. Twenty-two awards were handed out. The MVP of the major sports were Ken Starling for football, Doug Dailey for wrestling, and Randy Russell and Sharon Cable for basketball. Bob Corker and Ronnie Robertson received the coveted football Headhunter Award. Coach Davis showed a film clip of Corker, who was small in stature, making a crushing tackle on a much bigger back. After the clip, Davis exclaimed, "Now that's how you make a tackle!" Bob Corker also got recognized for his baseball skills by being named co-MVP with Freddy Hilliard.

The night concluded with the Dedicated Service Award for all sports teams, which went to Dr. J.J. Dobbs. Dr. Dobbs received a standing ovation for his medical care of all City High athletes. He was always around to help the Dynamo athletes. He treated many cuts, bruises, sprains, twists, and breaks.

Spook McKelvy was having a party at his house on the lake. His parents were out of town, so no doubt, it would be a wild one. A group of us had a round of pizzas and a couple pitchers of Coke at Pizza Hut and by the time we got to Spook's, there was already a good crowd. Spook liked soul music, which was blasting from the stereo. A rum punch was sitting in a small garbage can on the kitchen table. As the night went on, everyone seemed to be having a good time.

I'd been standing out on the back porch talking to Marvin Smith. Some kids called Marvin "Dude." I had no idea why, so I asked him. He told me his family owned the Dude Motel in Tifonia.

Suddenly, we heard a loud crash. It sounded like a tree had fallen in the living room. We rushed inside to see what had happened and there was Eddie Steakley standing over Chug Patterson. Chug was out cold with blood coming from a cut under his left eye. The whole left side of his face was already swollen. Chug was a big boy, as tall as Steakley and heavier by at least 50 pounds. They'd known each other since kindergarten and Chug was so easy-going, I wondered how he could get in a fight with anyone. I knew from football he was anything but aggressive. We never found out why Steakley hit him, but I was pretty sure that Chug hadn't been the aggressor.

It took a while for Chug to come to and when he did, he was still out of it. He didn't even know his name. So a couple of the guys took him to the hospital. He stayed there for two days with a severe concussion. It seemed like no party was complete without a Steakley fight. The sad thing was Steakley wasn't even invited. He just showed up.

At graduation, the class of 1970 turned over the keys to the school to the class of '71. The class of '70 had shown some good leadership. After all, we hadn't experienced any of the racial issues like at Brainerd and Central during the year. The last page of the Class of 1970 *Dynamo* yearbook summed up the social environment of our community pretty well:

"While our nation has been in turmoil and unrest, Chattanooga High has remained stable through the mutual love and respect shown by the faculty and the students. Both groups have worked in harmony to establish new customs to replace many of our old traditions. We have learned together to accept people as they are and not to pass unjustified judgment. We have been brought closer together as a school through the suffering of tragedy and again through the joy of victory. Throughout the year we have had the hand of God to guide us. ..."

We were now the seniors. It was up to us to show leadership as strong as the outgoing class as we began our last year of high school. We knew there would be challenges. We just didn't know what they'd be.

Chapter 32

Central's New Coach

After several months of waiting, the biggest question about high-school football was finally answered. Our cross-town rivals named Joe Lee Dunn to replace the legendary Coach Etter.

Joe Lee was a high-school All-American football player in Columbus, Georgia, and an honorable-mention little All-American at the University of Chattanooga. During his days with the Moccasins, Dunn played tailback, safety, and quarterback. Upon graduating from college, he returned to Columbus and coached high school. Then he went back to UTC as a coach, while completing his master's degree. He was very popular in Chattanooga during his playing days and this brought great excitement from the Central program.

But the road for Coach Dunn would not be easy. He was replacing a coaching icon, half the team was graduating, and the school was in a new and somewhat remote location. When Central was located in the center of the county, its teams attracted athletes from all over the eligible area. Kids who had traditionally gone to Central might now end up at other schools, such as Kirkman or City. In addition, the new school was building a football stadium, but construction was running behind and it was doubtful it would be ready for the upcoming season. Given all the changes, could the once-powerful Purple Pounders maintain their winning ways?

Time would tell, but meanwhile, school was out! It was the summer of our senior year, and we were going to have a blast! It wouldn't be all fun; some of us had to work. As for me, I either got a job or I'd be moving bricks in my back yard all summer long. Getting paid to work was a much better alternative and I landed a position as a bag boy at the Red Food grocery store in Dalewood. I was required to wear a white dress shirt with a red bow tie. I guess they thought it would impress the ladies who shopped at the store. My primary job was to bag groceries and carry them out to customers' cars. To my surprise, I was tipped for these duties. The standard rate was a quarter, but sometimes I'd get 50 cents, or if I was really lucky a dollar. I quickly found out that this was a great way to earn extra money. Smiling and saying, "Yes ma'am, thank you ma'am, and have a good day," became automatic responses when I carried the groceries to the car.

Most of the other guys on the football team also got summer jobs. Bill Wilder got a job at a YMCA summer camp. Lee Abelson worked for the Hamilton County school system maintenance department doing work that couldn't be done during the school year. Mike O'Neil bagged ice at the Tennessee Valley Ice Company. Bob Corker had worked there for the past two summers and had recommended O'Neil for the job. I guess you could say he had the coolest job in town.

Eddie Roberson's dad got him a job in construction as a brick layer. He worked on building the new North Gate Mall in Hixson. The job demanded long hours of mixing mortar and carrying brick for the masons. It paid him well, and he was always too worn out to get in trouble. That was probably his dad's overall objective.

Pat Petty spent most of his summer at the full-service Kayo gas station on Dayton Boulevard. Pat put in long hours pumping gas, cleaning windshields, and checking fluids; he even did some service work. His $1.60 an hour was good money, compared to the $1.45 I made at the Red Food Store. We all wondered why Pat worked so much. It would be almost a year before we learned the real answer.

Some of the girls also got jobs. Sammye worked at her family's Jo Ann dress store on Roseville Boulevard, which explained why she was always well-dressed. Cindy and some of the girls got a job at a *Chattanooga News Free Press* working on a cookbook for Helen Exum. The Exum family owned the paper and Mrs. Exum was fun to work for. But it was only part-time job, so babysitting and tutoring also supplemented her summer income.

I hadn't seen Cindy in a couple of weeks, so I wondered how she was doing. I still wasn't sure I was ready for a full-time girlfriend, but I did miss her. The summer was beginning, so working and having fun made it easier to forget her for the time being. However, some of our teammates and their girlfriends were going in a different direction.

Chapter 33

Wedding Bells Ring

While the rest of us were working, going to the lake, or just goofing off, a few had to deal with more serious issues. Most of us couldn't imagine getting married until we at least got out of college. We never considered the impact of being married as a teenager. Yet school had only been out for a few days when we heard that our kicker, John Cooper, was getting married to his high school sweetheart Angie Clark. Not only was John getting married, but he'd be a new daddy by the end of the year. John had handled all the kicking duties on the varsity the previous season and was expected to be a major factor for us in the fall. Although he said he was planning to play this year, most of us knew that the chances of that happening weren't good.

But Cooper's walk down the aisle wouldn't be the only one on the team. Unknown to the team or to the rest of the school, for that matter, Pat Petty had gotten married to his girlfriend Sharon Hudson. Pat and Sharon had dated since they were sophomores. She'd left school after the first semester of our junior year and had moved to Florida to live with relatives. She was due to have a baby in August. The marriage and the baby proved to be one of the best-kept secrets during our senior year. We wouldn't find out about this until the following April.

We had about a month before starting football activities. So work and play would be the order of business for the next 30 days.

The baseball players didn't get much of a break. If they wanted to be on the following year's team, they were required to play summer baseball. Coach Duke had a fairly demanding schedule, with local games during the week and road games on weekends scheduled as far west as Nashville and as far east as Kingsport, Tennessee.

They played other high-school, college, or American Legion teams, riding to the games with Coach Duke or parents. On one trip to Jefferson City, Tennessee, Mr. Gray took four boys with him in his new white Cadillac, which of course smelled like a new car. Kenny Smith asked to sit in the front seat of the car, claiming that he got car sick if he rode in the back. Of course, Randy S., Foster Yates, and Grant Hammond accused Kenny of just wanting to ride shotgun. So they loaded up the car, Foster got the front seat and Randy S., Grant and Kenny got in the back, with Kenny in the middle seat.

About an hour outside of Chattanooga, sure enough, Kenny got car sick. He couldn't get to a window, so he had no choice but to throw up on the floor of Mr. Gray's new car. The other boys were screaming and laughing at Kenny.

Mr. Gray pulled over to the side of the road and asked Kenny if he was all right. "Do you need to get something cold to drink?"

Kenny said, "No sir," then did his best to clean up the mess, but there was no way to get the smell out of the car. It was an unfortunate way to get rid of the new-car smell.

Mr. Gray said he'd go to a car wash and get the car cleaned up once they got to Jefferson City. So they rode the rest of the way with the windows down—and the other boys were glad to let Kenny ride in the front for the rest of the trip.

During these road trips, they rarely stayed in hotels or motels. It wasn't uncommon for them to play a double-header in the afternoon and drive home that night. Of course, during these drives, they listened to the Atlanta Braves on the radio. In those the days, the Braves were mediocre, but they were the

South's favorite—and only—team. So every town that had an AM radio station carried the Braves games. Milo Hamilton was the Braves radio announcer. He had a unique way of describing baseball. He could paint such a distinct picture of what was going on on the field that you could almost visualize every player's movement through the radio. A Dynamo infielder, Mike Gist, developed a fairly good imitation of Milo Hamilton's description of the game. Whether you were in the car, in the dugout, or at dinner, Gist provided whoever would listen with a "Milo" descriptive call of a game, or anything else for that matter—for example, a play by play of Foster Yates eating a cheeseburger. His teammates began to call him Milo. The nickname would stick.

When the team wasn't playing, the upcoming seniors were often over at Grant Hammonds' house. Marc and Mike Orr were regulars at the gathering. Grant lived with his mom in North Chattanooga, but she was rarely there, so it was a great place for the boys. The interior had a unique designer's touch. Grant's mom loved purple, so the interior had a purple motif throughout.

Arch and I continued to hang out a lot together. Arch talked a lot about football and how Coach Davis wasn't going to give him a chance. He was still mad about Davis's fifth-string comment during spring practice. I could tell Arch was going to do something. I just didn't know what it was.

Chapter 34

Summer Fun

When we weren't working, Arch and I went to the lake to hang out and water ski. I got off early on Wednesdays, so he picked me up at the Red Food Store and we headed up. On one ride, he told me that he and his dad had made a visit to Columbia Military Academy the week before. They'd met with the football coach, who assured him he'd get plenty of playing time in the upcoming season. Arch also liked the military environment. His dad, Arch Jr., had been in the Marines, so he grew up with a military influence. The upshot was that he'd changed his mind and was going there in the fall.

I told him that if he kept working hard, Davis would give him a shot. I continued by saying, "Arch, I broke my hand the first day of spring practice and missed the rest of spring. Hell, there are no guarantees I'll get to play either, but I'm not giving up!"

However, his mind was made up; he was going off to military school.

Of course, I told him once again he was crazy. But there was one more surprise in store for me: He'd convinced Ray Gorrell to go with him.

Now, I hated to see Arch go away to school, because he and I were such good friends, but to talk Ray into going with him was a major concern. Without Ray, we wouldn't have a party house! That was a *real* problem.

I couldn't understand why Ray wanted to go to CMA. He didn't even play football. Oh well, maybe Arch sold him a bill of goods about how many girls they could pick up in their military uniforms in Columbia, Tennessee. I'd had my fill of military schools and was glad to be a civilian, but if they wanted to live away from home and pretend to be soldiers, God bless 'em.

We skied till it got dark and then headed back home; I had to be at work at 7 a.m. the next day.

I got home from work at about 5:30 p.m. I'd just finished dinner when there was a knock at the front door. To my surprise, it was Kenny Smith. Kenny and I were friendly, but we didn't hang out together, so it was a real surprise to see him. I looked outside and saw Sammye's Mustang parked out in front. He said that he, Sammye, and Cindy were in the neighborhood and thought they'd stop by to see if I wanted to go with them to get some ice cream. I hadn't seen or talked to Cindy in three or four weeks and I hadn't been out with her since before the Junior-Senior Prom. So I said," Sure." I yelled to my mom that I was going out for a while and followed him out the door to the car.

I crawled into the back seat next to Cindy. I gave her a big smile and told her it was good to see her. She gave me a smile and a kiss on the cheek and said, "How have you been and what have you been doing?"

We took off and went to the Dairy Queen on Brainerd Road. Then we rode around Brainerd for a little while, just talking. I told Cindy what I'd been up to and gave her the update on Arch. We decided that the next night, the four of us would go to a drive-in movie.

The next night, they picked me up and off we went to the drive-in. It was a double feature. Fortunately, we had enough money that no one had to get into the trunk. Cindy and Sammye had learned their lesson about stowing away. We met some other friends there had a good time talking and cutting up. After all, we went to the drive-in to have fun, not to watch the double feature of Elvis's *Viva Las Vegas* and *The Return of Godzilla*.

After the ice-cream stop and the movie, Cindy and I began to see each other a couple times a week. When we didn't go out, she and Sammye were usually together. One night, they were on Signal Mountain, visiting a couple of classmates. When they headed down the mountain, they noticed that the gas gauge was on empty. They pulled in to a gas station, only to discover that neither one of them had any money. Looking under the seats and in the glove compartment, they came up with seventy cents. Fortunately, gas was only 28 cents a gallon, so they got almost three gallons in the car, plenty to get them home. It seemed like every time these two got together, they had an adventure. I was fairly sure it wouldn't be long before the next one.

Chapter 35

The Draft

Cindy's mom and dad had invited Sammye, Kenny, and me over for a cookout. Sammye and Kenny picked me up. At Cindy's house, Kenny and I stopped to chat with her dad, Clayton, who was outside at the grill, while Sammye went inside to see Cindy. Kenny couldn't tear his eyes away from the meat on the grill.

Clayton asked him, "Have you ever had a steak before?"

Kenny replied, "No sir." He came from a large family, so steaks weren't in the budget.

About twenty minutes later, Clayton brought the charcoal-grilled rib-eyes into the house. He handed them to Cindy's mom Catherine; she put them on plates with baked potatoes, green beans, and cornbread. Cindy poured everyone a glass of ice tea and we all sat down to eat at the dining-room table. Kenny cut into his steak, stared at the morsel, and took a bite. We all looked on as he tasted his first steak. Wide-eyed, he began to chew with great enjoyment. He exclaimed, "I've never had anything that tasted so good in all my life!" It was a great meal, one that I was sure Kenny wouldn't forget for a long time.

After dinner, the conversation moved on to Vietnam. Clayton had served in the Navy during World War II and had met Catherine while they were stationed in Jacksonville, Florida. She was a Woman Volunteer (WAVE), at that time the newly formed branch of women in the U.S. Navy. Clayton liked to talk about his time in the Navy. He worked on airplanes and kept them flying through the war. Now, he expressed his opinion about how the government had mismanaged the Korean and

Vietnam wars. He believed that if they let the generals run the wars, they'd have both been won in a hurry. He was very opinionated, so we just sat there and listened to his viewpoint.

Meanwhile, the need for soldiers was increasing. When a boy reached the age of 18, he was required to sign up with Selective Service, also known as the Draft Board. Boys were drafted based on age, school enrollment, profession, employment status, etc. The age range was 18 to 25.

The Draft Board had some discretion when it came to who was drafted. If your family had political connections, kids of draft age could get student, family, or job deferments. Other ways to avoid the draft were to join the National Guard or to get assigned to a non-military governmental job. Those who got drafted sometimes fled to Canada to avoid the war; they were called "conscientious objectors," meaning they were philosophically or religiously opposed to killing another human being. As you can imagine, those kids weren't looked upon with much respect, at least by those who were facing an overseas trip to the jungles of Vietnam or by veterans of prior wars.

Eventually, the War Department determined that the existing draft system was unfair to underprivileged kids. So to be fair to all, they inaugurated a lottery system.

The first draft lottery since World War II was held in December 1969. Boys born in 1950 would be eligible for the draft. The event was covered on radio and TV. It was like all lotteries: luck of the draw. Blue-plastic capsules containing every day of the year were placed in a large glass container. The order in which the birthdays were drawn established the order of the draft. The best number was 365, the worst was one. With the new lottery system in place, deferments and the like were now extremely hard, if not impossible, to get.

If it was your lottery year, watching the draft on television was a must-see. In the early years, the over-under number was around 100. In general, if your number was under 100, you had a good chance of being drafted. If it was higher than 100, chances were pretty good you wouldn't be going to war.

In 1970, Lee Abelson was 17 (and two years away from getting a "real" lottery number). He was quite interested in the draft, so he watched it closely. His birthday was June 8th. His birthday came up 7th in the 1950 lottery. Had he been born in 1950, he was sure to be drafted and his odds of a free ticket to Vietnam were excellent.

The war continued to be a daily topic on the national news, but we weren't too concerned about it in the summer of 1970. We wouldn't have to worry about being drafted for a couple more years. It was kind of like out of sight, out of mind. Our focus was on summer fun and the Fourth of July weekend was coming up.

Chapter 36

The Fourth of July

While some Americans were fighting in the jungles, the rest of the country was honoring the birth of our nation.

We were planning on celebrating the Fourth of July at the lake, especially when the hottest day of the year, at 101°F, was Friday July 3. After work Marc, Mike O'Neil, Arch, and I headed to Arch's lake property to spend the night and get ready for the Fourth. We cooked hot dogs and hamburgers on the open fire, then went out in Arch's boat and rode around watching the fireworks being shot off around the lake. We spent the rest of the night shooting the bull. Arch regaled us about Columbia Military Academy. I didn't say much.

The Fourth wasn't as hot as the day before, but it was hot nonetheless. Around noon, Cindy and the girls arrived to spend the day riding around in Arch's boat, skiing, swimming, and sunning. David Soloff joined us in a boat that was new to his family. It was a white and green "V" hull with an inboard-outboard Mercury engine. He also had his new girlfriend with him, Kim Fuge, who went to GPS. Anytime Soloff was around, we could expect a different level of craziness. So it was going to be a fun day at the lake.

The first order of business was to see which boat was faster, Arch's bigger blue tri-hull or David's "V" hull. Arch's boat also had a Mercury inboard-outboard engine. The race was from Arch's lake lot to Bass Bay, about five miles away on the Tennessee River channel from Chickamauga Lake. We all piled in the boats and cruised out of the cove at normal speed, so as not to rock the boat docks along the shoreline. But once we hit the channel, it didn't take long before both boats were running wide open.

Being a holiday weekend, there was a lot of boat traffic, which meant the lake water was rough. Rough or not, both boat captains were determined to arrive first at Bass Bay. Running wide open on choppy water could jar the teeth out of your head. About a mile into the race, the girls were yelling to slow down, but neither captain would hear of it. The first one to Bass Bay would have bragging rights!

Arch's boat was bigger and more powerful, while David's boat was small and could run closer to the shore. So Soloff cut the corners and kept up with the bigger boat as the tri-hull had to stay near the main channel to avoid running aground. The girls continued to scream as both boats bounced hard over the waves. Not only was it bone-shaking, it was also wet as the boats danced over the waves creating big plumes of water, some of which splashed into the boats, soaking the passengers.

About a mile from the finish line as Bass Bay Marine came into sight, Soloff had the lead, but shallow shoreline gave way to deeper water, so David's shortcut strategy was eliminated, with both boats now racing in the river's main channel. It was shaping up to be quite a sprint at the end. Soloff was about 100 yards ahead, but Trimble had a bead on him and was gaining. With a quarter-mile to go, Arch pulled up even with him and from that point, the race was over. Arch's crew sailed by Soloff and easily beat the white-and-green boat to the finish line. We all knew Arch would win, but David gave him a great run for the money.

We gassed up at Bass Bay, then split up, the boys going with Arch's boat to ski and the girls in David's boat to sunbathe at a nearby cove. Kim took the wheel of the "V" hull and we told them we'd be back in a couple of hours.

Outside the cove, Soloff got into the water, put on one ski, and was ready. The plan was to ski to the other side of the lake to a bigger cove where the water was smoother. This meant we'd cross the shipping channel.

Soloff pulled up and started gliding behind the boat. That was when we saw a barge chugging up the river. It was highly unusual to see a barge on the river on a weekend, especially a holiday weekend, but there it was, loaded with coal and riding low in the water, creating a tremendous wake.

I could see that devilish look in Arch's eye as he headed toward the barge. If the boat hit the wake just right, it would be like jumping a 12- to 15-foot wave. As we neared the barge, David hung on as he bounced over the choppy water.

About 50 yards from the back of the barge, Arch yelled, "Brace for impact!" He hit the wave at about three-quarters speed. It was like going up a hill. As he reached the crest, the boat shot completely out of the water, then slammed back down on the other side of the wake with a teeth-jarring boom. When we looked back to see where Soloff was, there was nothing but ski rope, still taut, but lost in the giant wave. David was missing in action!

All of a sudden, he shot over the top of the wave. His mouth was open and his eyes looked so big, I thought they were going to pop out of his head. He came out of the water, catching a good 10 feet of air; he seemed suspended for 10 seconds before landing safely on his ski with a big splash and a look of pure anguish look on his face.

But the wild ride wasn't over yet.

The boat was in the middle of the wake, with the other side of the large wave coming up. Once again, Arch headed up and over, Soloff hanging on, another time, for dear life and limb.

About 200 yards farther, Soloff dropped the rope and was finished with his first ride of the day. As he crawled into the boat, he looked at Arch and said, "I'll get you back for that, man."

Of course, we knew David loved every minute of the rare experience.

From the channel, we headed to the smooth skiing of the cove. We skied on two skis, one ski, and even boat paddles, just for the fun of it. After we'd skied a time or two, we headed back to where the girls were anchored. We split back up; David's crew heading off to Loret Villa Marina where his boat was stored and Arch's to his lake property. It'd had been a fun day, but now it was back to reality.

About midway through our skiing odyssey, my back was getting sunburned, but I'd left my shirt at the dock. Marc had an extra T-shirt, with the Budweiser logo, which I borrowed. At the end of the day, I told Marc I'd take it home and have it washed before I gave it back to him. When I got home, I threw the shirt in the dirty-clothes basket and promptly forgot about it. A couple of days later my mother washed the clothes and put the Budweiser shirt in a paper bag. The next day, I took Marc the bag. He pulled out the shirt, only to find a large hole in front where the Budweiser logo had been. We just looked at each other and started laughing. It hadn't occurred to me that Irene would be offended by it. I mean, she was a teetotaler and very anti-alcohol, but I didn't think she'd ever go to this extreme. Oh well, I told Marc I'd buy him a new one.

The Fourth of July was the turning point of the summer. We were just a week away from the beginning of football practice.

That week, the summer Dynamo baseball team finished up their season. They won the Optimist Tournament Championship by beating Riverside 12 to 0 in the final game. It somewhat avenged the loss to Riverside in the District Tournament during the regular season. With baseball season finally over, the players who also went out for football had only a few days to rest before they had to get back to work.

Chapter 37

Captain's Practice

The football team wasn't the only group gearing up for the new school year. The cheerleaders had been holding fundraisers most of the summer to spend a week at the American Cheerleaders Association Academy in Leesburg, Florida. Sheron Bunch, now the head cheerleader, was leading the group, along with Miss Ward, the cheerleader sponsor for Florida.

Unlike many other high schools, one of City High's traditions was boy cheerleaders. This year's squad had three: Ike Adams, Kurt Sisson, and Sidney Atkins. I sometimes wondered who were smarter—the boy cheerleaders or the football players. The football players played *for* the girls, while the boy cheerleaders got to hang out *with* the girls. The football players sweated and worked their butts off in order to play for the girls (and the fans), while the boy cheerleaders played *next to* the girls every day. They also got to be with the girls at the games, practices, and on road trips. Oh well, it was too late to worry about that now. My choice was already made and it was football.

Captains' Practice began the middle of July and lasted for three weeks or until it was time to start "real" practice, which was when high school football teams could start official training. The Captains' Practice was from four to six p.m. five days a week. For the most part, this allowed the players to continue working their summer jobs. The coaches weren't allowed on the field during the Captains' Practice, so they were theoretically run by the team captains. Bill Wilder and Joe Burns were the captains, so it was their show.

The real purpose of Captains' Practice was to begin to get the team in shape for the upcoming season. It was mostly for returning players, or new players who had the potential to play during the upcoming year. Basically, if you weren't a returnee from the previous year, you had to be invited by Coach Davis to attend. Since I'd played with the JV the previous fall and had been to spring practice, I was considered a returnee.

The daily routine was to meet with Coach Davis in the Armory before practice. He explained what he wanted us to do. Then, wearing T-shirts, shorts, and football cleats, we practiced on the lower field. Once we took the field, we started out with routine calisthenics. Then the linemen went to one end of the field, the backs and ends to the other end. Next we did some distance running with several laps around the track. The remainder of practice consisted of passing routes, punt fielding, or plays from our offensive play book. The session ended with running 10 sets of 50-yard wind sprints. Then sometimes, just for kicks, we ran sprints up and down the side of the hill.

Although the coaches weren't supposed to be around during the Captains' Practice, Coach Davis was always there observing. While working out on the lower field, we saw him sitting on the side of the hill behind a small tree and when we didn't do something the way he wanted it done, his voice boomed from behind the tree. Without showing his face, he barked out instructions.

At the conclusion of our outside work, we met again in the Armory, talked about what we'd done during the day, and reviewed the plan for the next day.

Now that Captains' Practice was in full swing, there wasn't much time for the lake, except on weekends. I normally worked on Saturdays, so Sunday was the best chance for us to go skiing. Once two-a-day practices began, the trips to the lake would be over for the year. So there was time for one more Saturday-night lake party, which would also be Arch and Ray's farewell party.

The usual crew got there after lunch on Saturday: Marc, Gary Seepe, Mike O'Neil, Marvin Day, David Soloff, and of course Arch and Ray. We spent most of the afternoon skiing. Soloff had the idea to cook a leg of lamb on the fire pit. When he got to the lake lot, he had a cooler full of beer and a frozen leg of lamb. He claimed he knew how to cook one and had planned the entire meal of lamb, potatoes, and French bread. That was good, since the only thing the rest of us had ever cooked on an open fire had been hot dogs on a stick.

Arch asked him, "How do you cook that damn thing?"

Soloff replied, "It's no big deal. You just cook it for about four hours and it needs to be on a spit that constantly turns over the fire."

Well, it sounded simple, but number one, we didn't have a spit, and number two, who was going to stand by the fire in the middle of July to turn the leg? I also got to thinking that we wanted to eat at eight, which meant we'd have to start cooking at four.

Predictably, we didn't get back from skiing until after six. We started the fire and rigged up a spit using tree branches and a metal rod we found in the trailer that didn't have too much rust on it. At about a 6:45, we put the lamb over the fire. We were all hungry from an afternoon of skiing, but until the lamb was ready, it was chips and beer. At about eight, the outer leg looked cooked and we trimmed off a thin layer of the lamb that was quite tasty.

As it was getting dark just after nine, the leg looked cooked from the outside. We were all thinking the same thing, "Maybe it only takes two hours to cook." The peer pressure was too great, so Soloff declared the lamb ready to eat and started cutting into it. We could tell it wasn't cooked, but we were hungry and had been drinking beer for the past five hours, so we would eat it whether it was fully cooked or not. The outer layer of meat was okay, closer to the bone was awfully rare, and the thick section was still frozen.

We sat around the campfire while we ate. Soloff had left the leg sitting on a piece of aluminum foil on top of a picnic table. An Irish Setter from one of the neighbors came strolling over. He sniffed around the fire pit and slowly walked over to the picnic table. We all sat there watching him as he looked up at the leg, then jumped up on the table, grabbed the lamb in his mouth, and took off running. We all just broke out laughing.

Someone yelled, "Looks like we better stick to hot dogs!"

The rest of the night we sat around drink beer, telling jokes, and poking fun at how cute Arch and Ray were going to look in their military uniforms. The next morning we all skied till mid-day, then went home. We had a great time and were sad to see Arch leave.

We entered the last week of Captains' Practice. We were anxious to go to the next step—three weeks of two practices a day. The beginning of August marked the time when all schools could start official football practice in preparation for the upcoming season.

There were big changes for a few schools in the upcoming season. Red Etter would be taking over the football team at the Baylor School. Central would have a new coach. Brainerd would try to recover from the racial unrest from the previous school year. As for City, the question was just how good would we be in Bob Davis's third year?

Chapter 38

The Cross Burning

As summer moved along, the Brainerd High School racial issues continued to be in the news. The school board had made a ruling that Brainerd could keep their nickname, the Rebels, but couldn't use the Confederate flag as a school symbol. They would also have to drop "Dixie" as their fight song. This was a crushing blow to some of the whites at the school, because they'd built up a tradition centered on this Southern heritage. For example, their football helmets featured the Confederate flag on the side. In the stands, numerous Confederate flags were waved during the ballgame. And of course, "Dixie" was played frequently—after a turnover, a touchdown, an extra point, etc. Before the games and during halftime, a female student, dressed as a Confederate soldier, rode a white horse around the field while carrying a Confederate flag.

Still, it was hoped that these changes, as well as a few other concessions, would mitigate the biggest racial issue in Chattanooga.

Up until this point, the public schools of Chattanooga had avoided forced busing to achieve desegregation. Most people, white and black, believed that forced busing wasn't the answer; they feared that it would destroy the schools and elevate the racial tension. Besides, the open-districting method used in Chattanooga seemed to be working. It allowed students to attend the school of their choice regardless of where they lived. In addition, schools consolidated through mergers or closures seemed to provide the balance needed for a peaceful integration.

The last Negro-only public school in the Chattanooga area, Chickamauga Elementary, had just closed at the end of the 1970 school year. Its students would be moved to Bess T. Shepherd Elementary at the beginning of the new school year.

In neighboring states, the integration movement wasn't progressing as well as it was in Chattanooga. The Nixon Administration was beginning to put more pressure on Southern states, where some 100 school districts continued to defy the Supreme Court desegregation edicts. After all, it had been over 15 years since the Supreme Court ruling in Brown v. Brown, which determined that the segregation of races in schools was unconstitutional. Certain school districts found ways to rebel against or slow down the integration movement. In Alabama, some counties had put in busing programs to comply with desegregation, but it might result in a daily 100-mile bus ride for some black children.

Resistance to desegregation was supported by some state governors. George Wallace of Alabama and Lester Maddox of Georgia were both staunch segregationists. In 1963, Governor Wallace made it clear where he stood on segregation during his inaugural speech. He said, "In the name of the greatest people that have ever trod this earth, I draw the line in the dust and toss the gauntlet before the feet of tyranny, and I say segregation now, segregation tomorrow, segregation forever."

Maddox campaigned hard for states' rights and maintained a segregationist stance while in office. In 1968 upon the death of Martin Luther King, Jr., Maddox denied the slain civil rights leader the honor of lying in state in the Georgia Capitol.

During the summer, it was reported in an article in the *Atlanta Journal Constitution* that Maddox urged Georgia parents to boycott public schools the first 30 days of the school year to protest the federal government's desegregation campaign. It went on to say, "Maddox bitterly labeled state school officials as cowards and challenged them to fight back at the tyranny of the federal government."

Marches, rallies, and protests continued throughout the South. In Georgia, thousands participated in a 120-mile march protesting the rights of blacks in the South and school integration.

Some of the neighboring counties reported Klu Klux Klan activities. On Saturday afternoon, it wasn't uncommon to see Klan members parading around town in their white robes and hoods, passing out fliers about white supremacy. The Klan was active around Chattanooga, as one incident demonstrated.

On a summer afternoon, several members of the City High basketball team were playing a game of pickup basketball in Gary Gaylor's driveway. Gary lived on Taft Highway, the main road across Signal Mountain. It leads from Chattanooga to Powell's Crossroads in Sequatchie County, where moonshining, cock fighting, and Klan activities could be found.

The Gaylors had a big flat driveway with a free-standing basketball goal on the side. The set-up made for a great half-court game. On that day, LeBron Crayton was playing. The boys thought nothing of it. LeBron was a teammate and a friend. Gee, everyone at City liked LeBron. He had a big part in the Riverside victory in February, which stopped their record winning streak. He was also one of the black student leaders at the school. He helped make the desegregation of City work, as opposed to the way it didn't work at Central or Brainerd. Other than the color of his skin, he was just one of the guys.

The boys played all afternoon, then sat around in the driveway and shot the bull, while enjoying cool glasses of lemonade.

That night after midnight, the Gaylor family was awakened by a bright light coming from the front yard. They ran to the window and pulled back the curtains and there, in front of their house, was a blazing cross.

By the time the police and fire department arrived, the cross had burned itself out. The police said that no doubt, it was the Klan. They asked a few questions about recent events at the house and Gary explained to them about the basketball game. The police officer told them that most likely, the Klan members were from Powell's Crossroads and had seen LeBron playing in the driveway on their way home from work in Chattanooga. The cross burning was their way to send a message, "No blacks on Signal Mountain."

Despite the Klan's efforts, segregation barriers were slowly coming down. But there was still a long way to go.

Chapter 39

The Boat Chute

The last day of Captains' Practice, we had our normal session. We were told to report at one p.m. the next day for physicals and to get our equipment. The following Monday would start the grueling two-a-day practice schedule, the last step before the start of the season.

On Friday afternoon after we finished with our physicals, I was laying out my equipment in my locker in the varsity dressing room. Coach Davis came around and asked me to stop by his office. I walked in and he told me that two black sophomores who were supposed to be really good players needed a ride to practice Monday morning. Reaumel Washington, a quarterback, and Vince Williams, a lineman, lived near Orchard Knob, just off Third Street. I drove down Third every day on the way to and from school and my house. It was one of the black sections of Chattanooga. He asked me if I would pick them up at 8 o'clock Monday at a small grocery store on Third Street. I told him I would, but wondered if I'd be okay. Generally speaking, white people didn't stop on this section of Third Street.

Saturday was my last day working at the Red Food Store. It also marked the last work day for most of the guys on the team. That night a bunch of us from City went to Lake Winnepesaukah a fun amusement park just south of Chattanooga over the state line in Georgia. I'd been going there since I was a small boy. Its featured attractions were the bumper cars, the Mad Mouse roller coaster with fast hairpin turns, the large Cannon Ball wood-framed roller coaster, and the Boat Chute. Of course, we also liked to spend time in the arcade, mainly playing Skeeball.

Cindy and I went with Sammye and Kenny. We met several other couples; Bill Wilder and Kathy Huffaker were there, as were Randy C. Gray and Susan Massey. There must've been another 10 or 12 City High kids there that night. We went from ride to ride, snacked on cotton candy and popcorn, and washed it down with ice-cold Cokes.

We had a few bumper-car rides. Then, saving the best for last, we headed to the Boat Chute, the first ride built at the park back in 1927 and the favorite for couples. The boat sat six people and started out in a dark tunnel about 100 yards long. It was pitch black, so couples could engage in a little romance. Of course, there were stories of water moccasins dropping into the boat from the tunnel's roof; there was even one story about a couple being bit and dying before they exited the tunnel. At the end of the tunnel, the boat climbed an 80-foot incline, then flew down a chute and hit the lake below, causing a great splash and soaking all the passengers.

The next day after church, I was invited to go to lunch at the Town and Country with Arch and his family. It was sort of his farewell party before he headed off to Columbia Military Academy in order to report to their two-a day practices. After lunch, I wished him the best of luck and headed home. I was going to miss Arch. I still found it hard to believe that he wanted to go to a military school for his senior year. He'd find out fairly soon that his lifestyle in Columbia, Tennessee, would be very different from the one he left in Chattanooga.

Chapter 40

Two-a-Days Start

At 8 o'clock on Monday morning, as instructed by Coach Davis, I pulled up in front of the grocery store on Third Street. I got a few strange looks from the folks milling around the store. I knew what they were thinking. "What's that white boy doing here?"

They found out soon enough, when two black kids dressed in gym shorts and carrying gym bags approached my car.

We introduced ourselves. Reaumel said his friends called him Mel, so it would be okay with him for me to call him that too. Vince was about 6'1" and weighed 240 pounds. I thought, "Damn, he's big for a tenth grader." Vince was fairly quiet, but Mel was quite the talker. He didn't stop talking until we got to the City High parking lot. We got dressed in our white practice uniforms and carried our maroon helmets down to the lower field. As we walked down the hill and rounded the corner, the field came into view. Despite it being the hottest part of the summer, the field was lush and green. The grass had just been cut and the smell of fresh-cut grass was in the air. The white chalk lines, outlining the 10-yard intervals of the field, were bright. But I knew that in a matter of an hour or so, the fresh grass smell would be replaced with the scent of dirt and sweat. Today, football would be serious business.

Coach Davis blew a whistle and yelled for everyone to join him at midfield. About 85 high-school boys dressed out in full football gear gathered around the coach. He said, "Get a knee."

Although everyone knew who they were, Davis went through the formality of introducing the coaching staff. Hubert

Smith was the defense's line coach, Claude Catron was the offensive line coach, and Buddy Guedron was our new end coach and would coach the defense. Coach Guedron replaced Coach Phifer. It went without saying that Davis was the head coach, the man in charge and the offense's coach.

Davis continued by saying that everyone had an opportunity to play on this year's team. Those who worked the hardest and did the best during the week would play on Friday night regardless of whether they were a sophomore, junior, or senior. He insisted, "Even if you're not a starter, you need to know the plays and the assignments."

On defense, he stressed learning how to read the keys and run the stunts when they were called. He said, "Guys, know what to do on every play, because you never know when you'll get put into a game. Everyone needs to be ready to play."

He continued, "Our goals this year are simple. We want to improve on last year's record and we want to beat Central. But don't worry about Central now! It's the last game of the year. We have to play nine other games before we get to them. For now, you need to know the plays and what to do in game situations. Beginning next week, our focus will be on East Ridge, since they're our opening game."

He said that he expected everyone to show up at practice on time. We had to keep our helmets on at all times during practice and while we were on the sidelines during games. The only time we could take our helmets off during practice was during water breaks or once we were off the field, heading toward the locker room. Hell, we even had to wear them during some of the team pictures.

He closed out the meeting by saying, "If you want to win, you have to work hard and if it doesn't hurt, it doesn't help. Okay, guys, let's get started!"

It was about 9:15 and already about 85 degrees with about 85% humidity.

The entire team lined up for calisthenics. After the exercise, we broke up into two groups. The linemen went to one end of the field and the backs to the other.

The linemen started out with log rolls. With three linemen side by side, at the whistle, one lineman dropped to the ground and rolled to the left. The next guy jumped over him and rolled. Then the third one followed. Once all three were on the ground, the first one popped up and the cycle continued until the whistle blew. This drill was supposed to help one's agility and replicate game action when a lineman was knocked down and needed to get up quickly to stay in the play. Then it was on to blocking drills.

The two-man blocking sled had a metal plate that sat on the ground and was about five feet square with the edges turned up. On the plate, a metal frame stood about four feet tall and protruded at an angle out in front of the plate by about three feet. On the structure, two "T" bars were affixed to each side of the frame. On the vertical part of the "T's," a pad was attached to them. Two linemen got on either side of the pads and when the coach blew the whistle, they hit the sled and tried to move it about 10 yards. The catch was Coach Smith was standing on the plate. He was about six feet six and weighed close to 300 pounds.

On the other side of the field, the backs also worked on a variety of drills, such as passing, tipped ball, ball carrying, and fumble prevention. Sometimes the passing drills were also the interception drills. A defensive back or a linebacker covered an end one on one as he ran a pass route. If the defensive player intercepted the ball, he was told to yell, "Oskee!" That notified the rest of the defense there had been an interception and they should now start blocking for the interceptor. Fortunately, I got to yell Oskee several times during the drill, although I thought, "Why 'Oskee'?" Why couldn't you just call, "I got it," like in baseball? Oh well, that was the football lingo at City High.

In the team drills, the linemen and backs worked together. The Oklahoma, made famous at the University of Oklahoma, was a contact drill between a lineman and a running back. They lined up three yards opposite each other. A running lane only about four feet wide used blocking bags on each side. There are a lot of versions of the drill; we ran a couple. In one, the running back stood up with his back to the lineman and the ball on the ground next to his foot. The lineman lay on his back on the ground with his head pointed toward the back. At the sound of the whistle, the back picked up the ball, turned, and tried to run by or over the lineman who'd rolled over and was now on his feet, trying to tackle the back. The drill ended when the ball carrier was tackled or the back ran past the lineman. When it came to my turn, I got into position and the lineman was on the ground. The coach blew the whistle, I picked up the ball, and spun around facing the lineman. I took a step to the left and made a quick cut back to my right and left, the defender grabbing air as I darted by him.

The other Oklahoma-style drill was with a defensive and offensive lineman and a running back. The ball carrier stood behind the offensive lineman. When the whistle blew, the linemen went at each other; the back, reading which direction the offensive lineman was trying to block, ran the other way. This simulated which hole the back should run through. If he got by the defensive lineman, the offense won, but if the defensive lineman tackled the ball carrier, the defense won. The defeated lineman, already embarrassed by getting beat, got more punishment by having to run a lap around the track immediately.

These Oklahoma drills were tough, but got the team energized.

We also did Bull in Ring. This drill also got the team all jacked up. There was yelling and shouting every time the coach blew the whistle for the next player to enter the ring. It was much tougher with the varsity than it was when I went against the JV players, but I fared pretty well, due to my quickness.

After the group drills, we got a five-minute water break. This consisted of lining up to get a drink out of the water hose at the end of the field. The water was hot and tasted like rubber, but it was still water. Then we broke up into offensive and defensive groups and ran through plays.

After the drills, the morning session consisted mainly of learning and running new plays. Finally, a couple laps around the track ended the morning session and we headed up the hill to the locker room—wringing wet from the sweat. We hung up our wet gear, in hopes it would dry out by afternoon practice. We had to be back on the field by 3:30. Vince and Mel were just going to hang out at the school in between practices. So I headed home for some lunch and a quick nap.

When we got back to the Armory, we dressed again for the second practice of the day. One of the team managers stood by the door handing out two salt tablets per player. I never quite understood the reasoning behind the salt tablets. After all, if you ate salty food, you wanted water to wash it down. Anyway, we were told that salt was supposed to keep you from getting dehydrated during practice, so doubts aside, we all took them and headed down the hill.

After calisthenics and backs and linemen drills, it was time for the daily scrimmage. The offensive and defensive teams split up and we began to run plays. Coach Davis worked with the offense, while the other three coaches worked with the defense. I started out working with the defense, since I was listed number one on the depth chart for one of the cornerback positions. I was number two on the offense chart as a running back. During the course of practice, I got to spend time running plays on both sides of the ball. I spent most of the time on defense and did well, making all the tackles that came my way. I only got to run about six plays on offense, but I made the most of them by making a couple of good blocks and getting nice gains the two times I ran the ball.

After the scrimmage, practice ended with 10 sets of 50-yard wind sprints. Then we headed up Cardiac Hill to the Armory. After two football practices in the summer heat and humidity, that was one long uphill slog.

With the first day behind us, I was happy with my effort. Now we had only 14 more days of these grueling two-a-day practices.

Above: Chattanooga High School

Below: The Troup

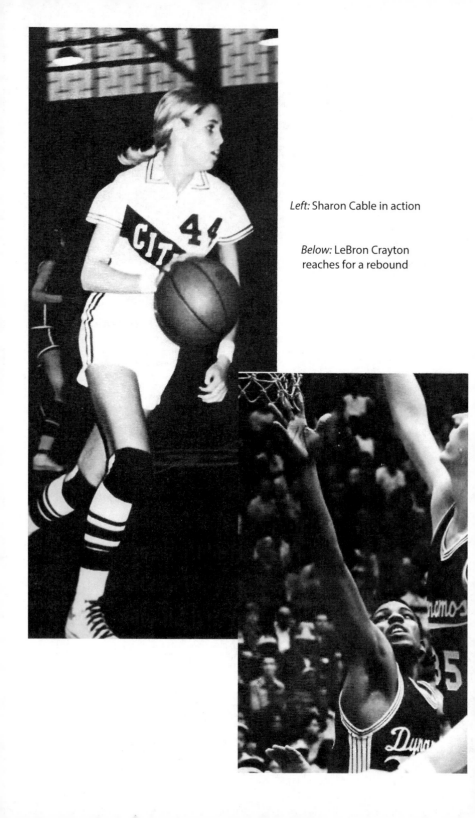

Left: Sharon Cable in action

Below: LeBron Crayton reaches for a rebound

Mike O'Neil and Coach Duke

The Tri Hi Y girls
(Cindy top row right side and Sammye in second row on the right)

Facing Page, Top: Buck Buchanan;
Bottom: The 1970 Dynamos

Sharon Bunch is crowned Homecoming Queen by Coach Phifer

Facing Page: Pat Petty and Coach Davis

Eddie Steakley goes up for a pass

Bill Wilder and Joe Burns with Coaches Catron and Guedron

Top: Eddie Roberson turns the corner headed for the end zone
Bottom: The starting backfield: Sanders, Roberson, Swanson and Wilder

Facing Page, Top: Denny Cornett with cheerleaders: Judy Alday, Susan Massey and Michele Medford; *Bottom:* Buck takes a hand-off from Wilder

Above: Bill Wilder gains yardage against Tyner

Below: Eddie Roberson returns a kickoff against Howard
with Buck running interference

Kenny and Sammye
Smith before a big date

The legendary coach, Red Etter

Below: James Lawson plows through the Central line

Above: Central players look on in dismay as Dynamos score again

Below: Coach Davis is carried off the field after victory over Central

Facing Page, Top: Davis consoles Coach Dunn after the game;
Bottom: Colonel Creed Bates leads the Snake Dance followed by
Dr. Henry and the student body

Cindy and Buck two years after graduation

The Buchanan Family in 2014

Chapter 41

Practice Goes On

While we were practicing football, once or twice a week Cindy, Sammye, and Sheron Bunch went to the lake house of one of Sammye's friends, Dr. Campbell. They spent the day sunbathing in colorful bikinis on the dock, floated around the inlet on plastic rafts, read teenage romance books, and talked about boys or gossiped about the girls around school. There was some discussion about college, but none of them wanted to think about life that far in advance.

By the second week, we were getting used to the tough regimentation of the practices. In the mornings as we walked into the locker room, the stench of dried sweat permeated the Armory. It didn't take long to find out that if you didn't wash your T-shirts and jockstraps frequently, they would dry in rigid form. A T-shirt worn for three or four days without washing could almost stand up by itself in your locker, thanks to the dried sweat. Some of the younger players found that if you didn't wear a clean jockstrap, a painful rash, or "jock itch," would develop. The school didn't have washers or dryers, so at the end of each day, most of us took our dirty laundry home and every morning brought back a clean T-shirt, jockstrap, and pair of socks.

If you could put up with the smell, you could wear your practice jersey and pants for at least a week without washing them. On Fridays we brought them home. Of course, our mothers didn't like that very much; most of us learned how to wash our own clothes if we didn't know how before.

Each morning if we were lucky, the sweat from the day before had dried out. If not, bright and early you were putting on wet, stinky, sweaty football clothes. Regardless, by the time the morning practice was over, if the pads weren't wet before, they certainly were by then.

Generally, after the morning practice, we showered, changed into street clothes, and headed home to eat, nap, and lounge around until the afternoon session, looking forward to getting into a wet uniform and shoulder pads.

The linemen were coached by Coach Catron and Coach Smith. Smith was a big but soft-spoken man. By contrast, Catron's mannerisms created fear among his players. He was an ex-Marine drill sergeant. We all tried to avoid his crew-cut hair and square-set jaw at any cost. He never smiled. He barked out orders. He made the linemen do the dreaded log rolls daily, which they truly hated. If a lineman screwed up a drill or a play, Catron made him run a lap.

One day after practice as we walked up the hill, Lee Abelson told me an interesting story about Coach Catron. The year before during Lee's knee rehab, he practiced on crutches and watched from the sidelines standing next to the ex-Marine coach. Right after he barked out a hard-ass order for his group to run laps, he turned to Lee, smiled, and even cracked jokes— just a regular guy. But as soon as the boys returned from their run, the coach was back to his stoic self. So he was somewhat human after all.

But the linemen weren't the only ones who had tortuous drills. The backs had their share of them. After we broke into group workouts, the defensive backs ran wind sprints backwards. These were run just like the last activity at the end of the day—except we back peddled for 50-yard intervals. We assumed the goal was to run as fast backwards as we could frontwards.

Dealing with the heat and humidity of summer practice

was always a challenge. It didn't take us long to figure out that drinking from the water hose wasn't the most pleasant way to keep hydrated. So most of us brought some form of fluid with us to drink immediately after practice. One unique trick was to get an empty gallon plastic Clorox bottle. Before it was used, it had to be cleaned and free of bleach. Next it was filled about three-quarters full with water, then put in the freezer overnight. (Clorox was about the only household product that came in a plastic container; everything else was sold either in glass or paper, neither of which worked very well when water was frozen in it.) The next morning, the water was frozen solid. We took it to practice and set it on the sidelines. The heat of the day melted the ice block and by the end of practice, we had a jug of ice-cold water.

Since I'd worked at the grocery store most of the summer, I'd discovered a new drink that was designed to quench one's thirst. It was a greenish-colored liquid by the name of Gatorade. It had been developed a few years earlier by a group of scientists who worked with the University of Florida's football team, hence the "Gator" in the name. Cold Gatorade was another favorite to quench one's thirst after a grueling day of practice.

Of course, after the morning practice, most of us drank excess amounts of fluid, so during the afternoon session, we were full and sluggish. The salt tablets didn't seem to help much, although the coaches insisted that they did. By the time we finished the afternoon wind sprints, almost everyone experienced a cottonmouth sensation. This was caused when your mouth had become so dry that it felt like you couldn't swallow. It was caused by the extreme heat and strenuous workout, from calisthenics and football drills to wind sprints.

After five days of hard two-a-day practices, we got Saturday and Sunday off. The following Saturday we were going to Mc-

Minn County for a scrimmage game. We were all excited about this; it would give us an opportunity to play another team and actually see how we were progressing.

The second week of two-a day-practices was pretty much the same as the first week. I continued to pick up Washington and Williams on Third Street. I found out that the year before, Vince had broken his leg playing football in Junior High. The break was above his knee and the doctor had told him that he would never play an active sport again. Vince would have none of that and was determined to play football again. He worked hard to rehab his leg. Amazingly, the doctors had cleared him to play. He sure didn't walk or run like he'd broken a leg. The two boys continued to hang out at the school between practices and Vince's dad picked them up after the second practice. As the days went on, I found out that stopping on Third Street wasn't that stressful after all.

Sometimes during the mid-day break, Mike O'Neil and Tommy Richmond came home with me to eat lunch. After lunch, we headed to the Shepherd Hills pool and sat in the water until it was time to go to practice. We found this to be quite refreshing during the hot days of summer.

School was still a few weeks away, but the City High campus was beginning to host more daily activities. Other groups were around school getting ready for the new year. The band, the drill team, the majorettes, and the cheerleaders now showed up most days. Like the football team, they were preparing for the upcoming season.

At football practice, we began to do less of the morning drills in order to focus more on game-style situations. We also worked on special-team plays: kickoffs, punts, extra points, and goal-line stands. These were in addition to the daily scrimmages.

The kicking game was a concern. Although John Cooper

said he was going to play this year, we all knew it was doubtful, due to the fact he was married and expecting a kid in a few months. John was rarely able to make practice, so Coach Davis began to look at other options. Several people tried their foot at punting and kicking. Three or four guys actually punted quite well. Even Soloff tried punting; he wasn't too bad, but it looked like Denny Cornett was the more consistent and would win the job. Eddie Roberson and I would be returning the punts. We both handled the ball well; plus, we were fast and elusive.

The field-goal kicking was another story. Many tried it, all using the straight-on kicking style. Soccer kicking was just beginning to be used by some pro football kickers and a few college kickers were trying it, but the straight-on kick was the norm for kickoffs, extra points, and field goals in high school. After a few days of tryouts, it looked like junior Ronnie Stinnett would get the kicking job by default. After all, he could put three out of five kicks through the goal posts. Even so, we hoped we scored enough touchdowns so we wouldn't have to rely on our kicking game in order to win. As for kickoff returns, it was clear that Roberson, David Sanders, and I would handle those.

Finally, John Cooper faced the fact that he could no longer play ball and told Coach Davis he had to quit. We'd miss him, but we understood.

The second week of two-a-day practices dragged on until Saturday arrived. We reported to the school at 8 o'clock in the morning. We dressed in our practice pants and boarded a school bus for the 60-mile drive to McMinn County. After an hour and a half on the bus, we pulled up to the school parking lot and unloaded, carrying our shoulder pads and helmets. We'd been issued old maroon jerseys to wear in the scrimmage.

Coach Davis played about 45 of us in that scrimmage. I played most of the game on defense and alternated at right halfback with David Sanders on offense. We weren't as big as McMinn County, but we were much quicker. They had a hard time keeping up with our speed. I caught a punt on our 20-yard line and zig-zagged back and forth across the field several times before I was finally tackled on their 30. It was a 50-yard gain, but I probably ran a total of a 100 yards during my circuitous route. Pat Petty came back to the huddle out of breath and said, "I finally gave up trying to block for you. Hell, I had no idea where you were going, so I can't take all the credit for that run. You did fifty percent of it on your own!"

We outscored them four touchdowns to one. It looked like we had a pretty good team in the making. As we boarded the bus heading back to Chattanooga, we were excited about the future of our football season.

Chapter 42

The Davis Way

We had one more week of two-a-day practices.

By now, it was fairly clear to me as to what kind of coach Bob Davis was. This was Coach Davis's third year at City High. He'd coached the seniors since his first year when they were sophomores. So this was truly his team and they were his players. His first team, in1968, went 5 and 5. The previous season, he led the Dynamos to a 7 and 3 record, the school's best since the '50s.

Bob, or Bobby as friends called him, was a football guy. He was 38 years old. He'd graduated from Meigs County High School and went to Tennessee Wesleyan where he played quarterback. After graduation, he became an assistant high school football coach. His first job was at Marion County High; from there he moved to Bradley County High, just up the road in Cleveland, Tennessee. His next stop was at Tyner High School, a Chattanooga-area school. Then his dream came true and he was offered the head coaching job at City High School. He'd always wanted to be a head football coach. He felt that City was a great place to build his football legacy, since it didn't have a strong football tradition, but it did have a strong school tradition and a long respected history. He could put his own stamp on the program.

He was a traditional-type coach. He liked tough hard-hitting teams. But his basic strategy was also based on being nimble and fast. He didn't believe in running a lot of gimmick plays; a halfback pass or a reverse was as extreme as he got. He also favored standard football formations. We ran a straight "T" formation. The "T" had a center in the middle with guards, tackles, and ends to each side, spaced about two feet apart. In the backfield, the quarterback was under center and the fullback was three yards directly behind him. At an arm's length away to each side of the fullback were the halfbacks. When he wanted a different offensive look, we flanked out one of the backs by one of the ends as a wingback. From the "T" we ran about 15 different plays. He insisted that we run them well. In practice, we ran these plays over and over until he was satisfied that we had them right. On defense, we ran a simple five-two set: nose guard, two tackles, and two ends, with two linebackers, a rover back, two cornerbacks, and a safety.

When it came to football, Davis was all business. We studied films of games the team played last year and film of teams we'd be playing this year. He pointed out an opposing team's tendencies, which would tip their hand as to the next play. He ran that 16mm projector daily and studied those black-and-white films by running them forward and backward time and time again. As much as he used that projector, he probably wore it out during a season.

On the field, practices were structured and organized. We knew what we were going to do before we got there. During practice, he provided instructions to correct mistakes. If a player did something wrong, he never belittled him; rather, he simply corrected his error. Yes, he got emotional and excited and he yelled, but it was all in the service of making a boy better, rather than making him feel bad about himself. He tried to build self-confidence in his players.

Once during a two-a-day practice, it seemed like we couldn't do anything right and had no enthusiasm. He called us together. "Guys, you don't want to be here today, do you? Your minds aren't on football and you're wasting my time. Let's just call it quits. Let me know when you're ready play football again!" He turned and started walking away.

We knew he was disappointed in our lackluster effort. We all looked at one another and knew we had to do better and get him back on the field. So we yelled at him and told him that we wanted another chance.

But then he played the hard-to-get card. "You all don't have it in you."

Hell, we almost had to beg him to let us keep practicing.

He finally agreed and we restarted practice. His psychology worked and as you might expect, it turned out to be one of our best practices of the summer.

He seemed to be able to draw out the best in a player. It was the way he talked to us on and off the field. He was a straight-forward man and told you what was on his mind, but he also had a sense of humor. He used catch phrases to get his point across. He preached, "Always know the down and distance!" Sometimes when someone missed a tackle, he yelled, "If you're scared, holler scared!" Of course, he used his favorite slogan often, "If it doesn't hurt, it doesn't help!"

Coach Davis believed that the team was more than a bunch of individuals. He preached teamwork and stressed the fact that 11 boys playing together was a hard combination for anyone to beat. He also had the ability to bring a diverse group of guys together as a team. Our team was made up of boys from all over the county—whites and blacks, wealthy and poor, Protestants, Catholics, and Jews. But when it came to playing football, Coach Davis got us to leave these differences at home, because he instilled in us that once we hit the field, we were no longer individuals. We were part of an entire team's effort.

This year's team had six black kids on the varsity: Washington, David Sanders, Charlie Smith, Artis Young, Vince

Williams, and Marvin Scott. Only Sanders would be a starter, but all would see some action. We never thought anything about their skin color; they were teammates and only teammates. In Davis's eyes, you had to prove yourself on the field. He started imparting this to us at the first winter workout. We'd play as a team and put the best team players on the field. The team would work as one and we would be winners.

Davis also believed the team had the right to make its own decisions. Even though he was the guy in charge, he wanted the team to vote on issues. When it came to discipline, he let us decide who would stay and who wouldn't. On the trip back from the scrimmage at McMinn County, Pat Petty and Artis Young, a black kid who played guard, got into a fight on the bus. The two of them had been playing against each other during most of the two-a-days. Both were intense on the field and there were a few shouting and shoving matches over the past couple of weeks. For some reason, it just came to a head on the bus ride home.

The fight was broken up, but when we returned to the locker room, it resumed. It took four or five of us to pull Pat off of Artis. Without a doubt, Pat had gotten the better of him.

After the fight, Coach Davis called both boys into his office and told them not to come back to practice until they were ready to apologize to each other and the team. He emphasized that this was no way for teammates to act. "It's okay to fight the other team, and fights that flare up during practice are part of football. But fighting between ourselves on the bus or in the locker room will not be tolerated."

When Monday morning practice rolled around, Artis showed up and told Coach Davis that he was sorry and wanted back on the team. Coach Davis called the team meeting and asked for a vote. The team voted unanimously to reinstate him. But Pat Petty was nowhere to be found.

Pat was still mad about the fight and didn't show up at Monday's practice. In fact, after the talk Coach Davis gave him, he was ready to quit football once and for all. Pat was one of the emotional leaders on the team. He gave 100% and expected everyone else to do so. But Pat was also dealing with some serious personal issues off the field. At the time, no one on the team or at school knew that just days before, Pat's wife Sharon, whom he'd secretly married at the end of the 1970 school year, gave birth to a baby boy in Florida. Every day, Pat had to think about what he should do. Should he be with his wife and baby, quit school, and get a job? Should he stay in school and graduate? Should he give up football? All were tough decisions for a 17-year-old high school senior.

Pat took two days to think about it, then came back to Coach Davis, apologized to Artis, and asked the team if he could rejoin. The apology was gladly accepted by all parties. We were pleased and relieved that Pat changed his mind, because his drive and spirit made us a better team. Yet, even though Pat was a key player, Davis held his ground on his decision.

Although Davis was all about winning, he had rules that had to be followed to play on his team. He believed in keeping the approach simple. Follow the plan and you'll be successful. Everyone on the team has a job to do and if everyone does their job, we'll win. He developed a winning attitude and a winning environment. To him, if you were in a football activity, it was serious business and not time for playing pinch-butt and grab-ass!

This was best illustrated on picture day, when we wore our new uniforms and had team, group, and individual pictures taken for the season programs and the school yearbook. We practiced only in the morning; the afternoon was just for the shoot. So it was more or less an easy day.

As we were assembling for the team picture, one guy playfully joked with a teammate and before he could turn around, Coach Davis had slapped his shoulder pads and got up in his face. "Don't ever let me see you laugh on a football field again. Nothing is funny about football!"

The coach's red twisted face showed how sincere he was about proper behavior in a football setting. The scared look that crept down the player's face was enough to let everyone know that respect for the game was now key for City football.

When it came to the game, Davis knew both sides of the ball, but his focus was on the offense. He developed the offensive play book. In essence, in addition to being head coach, he was the offensive coordinator. He called every play during games. We all knew he had a game plan that if we executed, we would win. When game time came, we were confident that we had the best coach on the field.

Coach Davis's move to City had been a good career move. This was only his third year and he'd just been appointed the new Athletic Director for the school, in addition to his head-coach duties. This was a result of recent changes in the administrative staff of the school district. Dr. Jim Henry, the principal last year, had moved on to become the Superintendent of the Chattanooga Public Schools. Coach Jim Phifer, who had been the Athletic Director, assistant football coach, and head basketball coach, was promoted to principal.

We could tell that Coach Davis was excited about becoming the leader of Dynamo athletics, but it was clear to all of us that his real passion remained football. He thought about it year-round. Although it was illegal to recruit, he did have ways to get players into the program. Vince and Mel could have gone to Riverside, which was only a couple of miles from their homes, or any other school in the Chattanooga area, but somehow Davis convinced them to come to City. Then he found Lee Abelson as a sophomore, when his only involvement with football was making signs for games, and convinced him to come out for the team.

He also believed in developing players. He set up sophomore and Junior Varsity teams and scheduled games for both teams. This allowed players to get game experience whatever their skill level. So by the time a player got to be a senior, he'd played in 10 to 20 games. That experience was valuable in the Davis strategy.

We didn't know much about Coach Davis's personal life. All we knew, and needed to know, was that he was our coach and he would make us winners! He had three basic maxims, which he instilled in us. These were:

Play as a team.

Work at it until you get it right.

If it doesn't hurt, it doesn't help.

Most of us took these principles with us and would hold them dear for the rest of our lives.

Chapter 43

The Last Week of Two-a-Days

Two-a-days were almost over and school would be starting soon.

The afternoon scrimmages were fairly intense. There was a lot of hard hitting; the players knew it was the last time to make a good impression on the coaches.

About halfway through one of the last the inter-squad scrimmages of the summer, Eddie Steakley went down with a shoulder injury. He left practiced and went to see Dr. Dodds.

The word came back from the doctor that Steakley had a broken collarbone and couldn't play for four to five weeks. This was a big blow to our offense, because he was our best receiver. He was bigger than most of the defensive backs we'd play against, so all Bill Wilder had to do was throw the ball up high and Eddie would haul it in. If there was tight coverage on him, Steakley used his basketball experience to get position on the defensive back. In essence, he just "boxed out" the defender, no different than going for a rebound on the basketball court.

Our last scrimmage against another school was when Notre Dame came to us. The grass had been cut earlier in the day in the field had been lined off with new chalk. The Irish had had some issues earlier in the summer when 19 of their players failed to show up at the beginning of training camp, which was held at Camp Columbus up by the lake. Apparently, they were disgruntled with one of the coaches. Parents, school officials, and the coaching staff got together and after a week of being "on strike," the 19 players came back to the team.

It was clear that we were the better team on the field that day. Our defense prevented them from gaining any significant yardage. Offensively, we moved the ball steadily down the field. About 45 or 50 players saw action that day. Afterwards, we felt very good about our chances in the upcoming season. After the way we played against the two schools in the scrimmages, we had a lot of confidence.

The next day, it was back to our normal routine. In the afternoon scrimmage, Denny Cornett was alternating with Eddie Roberson at left halfback. Cornett took a hand-off from Wilder and was hit hard in the hole by two linebackers, really jarring his neck. Denny was slow in getting up. Two plays later, the same play was called with the same results, but this time Denny stayed on the ground with a grimace on his face as he rubbed his sore neck. The coaches looked at him and told him that he should go see the doctor and get it checked out.

After practice, Eddie Roberson volunteered to take him to the doctor. Although Eddie and Denny were technically competing for the same position on offense, it was fairly clear that Eddie would open the season as the starting left halfback, though Denny hadn't given up the job just yet. They headed to Dr. Dodds's office. Denny's neck was really hurting and every time Eddie hit a bump in the road, it caused him additional pain. In Denny's mind, it seemed like Eddie was trying to hit every bump on purpose. The doctor determined that he only had a neck sprain and shouldn't have contact for a week. And once he came back, he should be fitted with a "horse-collar" pad attached to his shoulder pads to give his neck more support.

The two-a-day practices ended and we were all glad. It had been a tough three weeks. Coach Davis announced the starters. I'd earned a starting position on defense as the right cornerback, the position that Bob Corker had played the year before. I'd also run back punts and kickoffs. In addition, I'd see time on offense as the second-string running back.

After a year away from football, I'd earned a starting spot on the varsity. Football was here and I was back in the game!

Chapter 44

The Jamboree

The Jamboree was the official kickoff of the 1970 high school football season. Our focus was on football and the Jamboree, but the City of Chattanooga was concerned about its icon, the railroad.

From before the Civil War until 1970, Chattanooga had been known as a railroad town. The famous song, "Chattanooga Choo Choo," made Track 29 come to life. The song was written during the heyday of the railroad passenger service in the country, and Chattanooga gained worldwide recognition as the hub of this glamorous mode of travel.

The newspaper reported that the Southern Railroad Train Station on 1434 Market St. would be closing. The terminal opened in 1909. For over 60 years, this terminal had been a center point of the Chattanooga economy and society. Freight trains would continue to utilize the Chattanooga network of tracks, but the days of passenger service officially ended when the *Birmingham Special* left the legendary train station for the last time. The city made famous by trains now had to look for a new industry to identify with.

The Jamboree was a two-night football exhibition played at Brainerd High. It featured 16 teams that played eight short games lasting only one quarter, which was 12 minutes. There were four match-ups on Friday night and four more on Saturday. The first game started at 7:30 p.m. the last one at 9. The point of the event was to give fans a taste of football and the opportunity to see what their teams looked like for the upcoming season. The Dynamos played the last game on Saturday night.

So Friday night, most of us went to Brainerd to watch the games and get some idea about the competition.

On Saturday afternoon, we reported to the Armory and were issued our maroon game uniforms. After getting our ankles taped, we dressed in our pants and T-shirts. We had a brief meeting about the game plan for the night. Then, carrying our shoulder pads and helmets, we headed to the parking lot.

The 1970 Dynamo varsity football team boarded a yellow Chattanooga Public School bus and took off to Brainerd High. The crowd this night was expected to be larger than the night before, since it featured the home-team Rebels, our opponent. Last year, Brainerd had finished the season undefeated and was ranked second in the state. Everyone was anticipating a close contest.

We got the ball first. It was Lee Abelson's first varsity action after sitting out the entire previous year with his knee injury. The first play was a run. Lee fired off the line, making his block, and Eddie Roberson gained seven yards. But Lee took a knee to the head and went down like a rock. He finally got up, but was wandering around like he was lost and started heading to the Brainerd huddle. Tommy Richmond, the left guard, grabbed him by the jersey and pulled him into our huddle. Before the ball was snapped for the next play, Lee turned to Tommy and asked him in a soft voice, "Who do I block?" Tommy told him. After another successful running play, Lee got off the ground and followed Tommy back to our huddle.

We drove the ball down the field with a methodical running attack. All three of our running backs surged for significant gains. With the ball on the Brainerd seven yard line, Roberson took a pitch left and rounded the end, heading to the goal line, but he was hit hard at the three yard line. The ball popped out of his hands and bounced into the end zone. Fortunately, Mike

O'Neil, playing right end, was in the right spot at the right time and pounced on the loose ball for a Dynamo touchdown. We converted the two-point-conversion play and led 8 to nothing. We had chewed up a lot of time and driven the ball 70 yards in 14 plays.

After our score, Brainerd got the ball, but we didn't allow them to get a first down, so they had to punt to us.

We continued to run the ball and when the final whistle blew, we'd rushed for over 100 yards in the 12-minute game. We'd played well and had beaten a rival. Our excitement levels continued to rise.

On the bus, we learned that, apparently, Lee had been knocked out on the first play from scrimmage and didn't remember anything about the game. Tommy had to tell him what to do on every play. Most likely, Lee suffered a concussion, but he kept on playing. The coaches didn't even think about concussions unless you were knocked out cold.

As we crossed the Tennessee River, I gazed out the window and for a few moments I tuned out the chatter and thought, "I'm back on the field. It's been a long wait." It felt good.

Back at school, we all grabbed quick showers and headed out to an end-of-summer party on the mountain. Next week school started. The first game of the season was on Friday night at East Ridge and we were ready.

Chapter 45

Kickoff Time!

The first day of school was cool, because you got to see friends you didn't see during the summer. I got to school early and met some of the guys under the clock in the Commons. This year was a whole different story for me than last year. Now I was one of the guys sitting under the clock, instead of the new guy wondering who the clock guys were. Marvin Day got there earlier than anyone else and claimed the prime position in the chair sitting directly under the clock. He would maintain that position all year.

Our position under the clock was a great place to view the new students. Of course, the big attraction was the sophomore girls. Some of the guys were already talking about them and giving us the rundown.

As we entered the school, we were greeted with signs about the upcoming game against East Ridge. During the activity period, the entire student body attended the assembly in the auditorium. Coach Phifer was now the principal; he gave an overview of the upcoming year. He talked about the previous troubles at Brainerd and Central and said that he didn't expect any problems at CHS, thanks to the progressive attitudes of the City High students. He then introduced the faculty, followed by the senior-class officers: Lee Abelson was the president, Bill Wilder vice president, Rosie Raulson secretary, and Joni Knight treasurer. Next, Phifer had the coaches or sponsors introduce the captains of each of the sports teams, along with the majorettes, drill team, band, and cheerleaders. The captains of the basketball teams, Mark Eaton and Sharon Cable, gave an entertaining display of their basketball skills. At the end of assembly, the cheerleaders led us in a few enthusiastic cheers about beating East Ridge! The assembly ended on the upbeat and we return to our next class.

My last year of high school, I had a normal load of English, Spanish, math, history, and mechanical drawing, all the classes I needed in order to graduate. Sixth period was designated physical education, which really meant football practice. My focus was almost entirely on football.

That night at home, I got a call from my buddy Arch. He told me that he'd be the starting wingback and cornerback for Columbia Military Academy. Their first game was Friday. We chatted a little while about how things were going, then I wished him the best for the season.

In Chattanooga, during this time of year, the two newspapers' sport pages focused on Tennessee, UTC, and high school football. Baseball was fading; the Braves were out of the running for the pennant and the NFL's Atlanta Falcons expansion team was still a struggling franchise. So there were daily articles on the local football activity. Most of the writers picked City to be one of the top teams in the region. Although we had a lot of new faces on the team, we seemed to have a bunch of guys who worked well in the Davis system. We'd also performed well in the two preseason scrimmages and the Jamboree.

We seemed to get more press coverage in the *Chattanooga News Press* than the other high school teams. Two of the sports writers gave us a lot of attention. Roy Exum was a sports beat writer who had graduated from City and Ward Gossett was a young intern who was assigned to help with the coverage of high school football. Ward was going out with one of our girl basketball players, Becky Dillender. We saw both writers a lot.

Roy and Coach Davis had become big buddies. Roy's younger brother Jon was a senior at City.

We practiced all week getting ready for the Pioneers. On Monday afternoon, we watched game film of them from last year. Davis pointed out their key players and their favorite plays, plus some trick plays they liked to run. For the next three days, the JV team ran the plays we expected East Ridge to run on Friday night.

The Thursday practice was the final prep day for the East Ridge game. We headed out to the upper field in helmets, shoulder pads, and shorts for some last-minute instruction. There was no hitting; we just ran through blocking assignments and defensive positions that we planned to use against East Ridge. We also went through the various special assignments, so everyone knew where to go for punts, kickoffs, and extra-point tries. At the end of practice, Coach Davis gathered us together to review the schedule for Friday. He told us to eat a hearty meal before we arrived at school no later than 5 o'clock. We needed to be dressed and ready to go by 6.

Friday arrived and we were ready to play football. It was hard to focus on school work, because of our excitement. All the football players wore their game jerseys to school. During the assembly that afternoon, we had a pep rally. The football players were introduced onstage and Coach Davis gave a short summary of the upcoming season. The band played and the cheerleaders led the student body in loud rounds of cheers. The much-anticipated season was almost here and the entire school was excited over the prospects for this year's Dynamo team.

I got to school just before 5. All backs were required to get their ankles taped. Of course, that meant we had to shave our ankles. Otherwise, you'd rip the hair off your legs when the tape was removed and that was like some kind of Chinese-torture treatment. So I shaved my ankles the night before. It looked weird with no hair below the sock line.

After getting taped up, it was time to go. Carrying our helmets and should pads, we boarded the yellow school bus and headed to East Ridge. Not a word was spoken on the way to the stadium. All the players were focused on what their jobs would be once they hit the field.

We didn't notice that the sky was getting darker and darker as we moved westward. But we got off the bus into a hot muggy night with the smell of rain in the air. The weather man had forecasted light showers for later in the evening, but we paid no attention to it. We just wanted to play.

The game was scheduled to kick off at 7:30. At about 6:45, we left the locker room and went out on the field for warm-ups. We could see that the stadium was nearly full. Our band, drill team, and cheerleaders were there as well. Excitement was in the air!

My dad and mother were there. Irene had only seen me in one other game, at Castle Heights. She was always afraid I was going to get hurt. It just made her too nervous to watch me play. E. Blaine, on the other hand, liked football and didn't miss a game. He even came to some of the practices during the week. He loved it when I made a tackle, a crushing block, or a good run. In his mind, the tougher the game, the better. He didn't worry about me getting hurt; he just wanted me to make the play.

About halfway through our warm-ups, the storm rolled in. Bright streaks of lightning lit up the sky, followed by loud cracking thunder. The lightning flashed all around us as the rain began to pour down. We were told to go to the locker room, from where we could hear the thunder booming outside. After about 45 minutes, one of the officials came in to talk to Coach

Davis; the game had been postponed until tomorrow night. A disappointed group of football players headed to the bus for the ride back to the Hill. I wondered, "Will I ever get to play in a real game?"

Saturday morning, E. Blaine took it easy on me and didn't assign me any chores for the day. So I slept late, got up, ate breakfast, and read the sports page. Apparently, our game was the only one that was cancelled. The college season also started on that day. Ole Miss, led by Archie Manning, was picked to win the Southeastern Conference. Tennessee was also expected to do well. In the afternoon, I watched the college football game of the week on TV, then headed out.

The weather forecast was good: very hot, but no rain.

We went through the same routine as the day before, once again boarding the bus bound for East Ridge. Except this time in the locker room, Davis again reviewed the key points of the game. Then he asked us, "Are you ready?"

A roaring, "Yes, sir!" was the response.

"Remove your helmets, grab a knee, and recite with me."

"*The Lord is my shepherd; I shall not want. He makes me lie down in green pastures. He leads me beside still waters. He restores my soul. He leads me in paths of righteousness for his name's sake.*

"*Even though I walk through the valley of the shadow of death, I will fear no evil, for you are with me; your rod and your staff, they comfort me.*"

We only said the first two verses, then Coach Davis added his own prayer, something along the lines of, "Keep everyone safe and uninjured in the game tonight." After the "Amen," we gave another loud round of yells and stormed out of the locker room and on to the field.

We congregated at the visitor's sideline and were ready to play. We won the coin toss. The East Ridge band, clad in orange uniforms, was on the field. The public-address announcer asked everyone to stand and remove their hats. A local Baptist preacher said a prayer, then the East Ridge band played the national anthem. At the end of the song, the entire stadium cheered and we headed on to the field.

Our band, drill team, majorettes, and cheerleaders were there ready to cheer us on. The band was decked out in their new uniforms, which looked sharp.

As we lined up for the kickoff, I noticed that the stands were packed and people were standing all around the field, shoulder to shoulder, four or five deep. The game was sold out and I learned later that it was estimated over 7,000 people were in attendance.

As the East Ridge kicker set the ball on the tee, Eddie Roberson and I went back to the 10-yard line, ready to receive the kickoff. The referee blew the whistle, the kicker kicked the ball, and everyone in the stadium cheered as our football season finally got underway. Eddie fielded the kick and ran it out to the 30-yard line. After one first down, our drive stalled out.

The Pioneers weren't able to move the ball either. The rest of the first quarter was a back-and-forth match with no scoring.

In the second quarter, I intercepted a pass to stop an East Ridge drive. We drove the ball down the field and scored on a short run by fullback John Swanson. We kicked the extra point and led 7 to 0.

On the next series, East Ridge countered with their own drive. They scored on a passing play and made the extra point, which tied the game at seven.

We took the kickoff and began to move the ball, but Eddie fumbled about midfield and East Ridge recovered.

The Pioneers drove the ball down the field, but we stopped them at the 20-yard line.

On fourth down, Mitchell kicked a field goal and the half ended with the Pioneers leading 10 to 7.

Chapter 46

Davis Goes Down

Halftime came and rather than going to the locker room, Coach Davis told us to go to the east end zone. It was a very hot and humid night and it would be cooler in the open air than in the stuffy locker room under the home stands. That was a good thing, since we'd had spent a lot of time in the place the night before.

The defensive group sat on the ground drinking water or Gatorade as we listened to Coach Guedron reviewing our defensive play of the first half.

After about 10 minutes, we heard some commotion coming from the offensive group, about 30 feet away from us. We looked around to see Bill Wilder leaning over Coach Davis, who was lying on the ground. We all started heading that way, but the other coaches stopped us, telling us to get away and give Coach some air.

We could see the coach's eyes were closed and beads of sweat rolled off his face. Fortunately, Dr. Dodds was with us and he promptly began attending to the coach. Apparently, he'd become nauseous while waiting for the band to get on the field for their halftime performance.

An ambulance was called, but it would be 30 minutes before it arrived. Someone suggested that he be taken to the hospital in a car, but Dr. Dodds told everyone to stay calm and wait. Davis wanted to walk to the bench and watch the rest of the game, but again, Dodds insisted that Davis remain still.

The ambulance finally arrived. The paramedics put Coach Davis on a stretcher and loaded him into the back. Dr. Dodds got in the ambulance with the coach and off they went.

The word was he had suffered a heart attack.

The whole team was in a state of shock. Our head coach, our offense coordinator, our play caller, and our leader was on the way to the hospital in the middle of the first game of the season!

The Davis situation had caused about a 45-minute delay in the game. It was now time for the second-half kickoff. We all gathered around and Eddie Roberson said a prayer, asking God to watch over our stricken coach. At the end, we all chimed in with an Amen.

The three remaining coaches were joined by Coach Phifer, our new principal, who was our end coach last year. Phifer told us not to worry about Coach Davis, that he was in good hands and would be all right. Coach Catron, now the acting head man, told us to focus on the game and run Coach Davis's plan. The problem was the game plan was with Coach Davis, who was in the back of an ambulance. Coach Catron and Coach Guedron called the plays.

It was hard not to think about Bob Davis.

East Ridge got the ball first and we stopped them, forcing them to punt. Eddie caught the booming kick inside our 10-yard line. After a dive play up the middle for a loss of two yards, we tried a sweep to Roberson. The Pioneers must have known it was coming; they crashed in on the left side and met Eddie at the goal line. He reversed his direction and they tackled him in the end zone for a safety. The Pioneers now led 12 to 7.

We kicked to them from our 20-yard line and stopped them the rest of the game.

Our offense got the ball inside their 20-yard line three times in the second half, but couldn't push it across for the score. Once we got near the goal line, it seemed like we didn't know which play to run and we blew it. The coaches as well as the players seemed lost and confused in the shadow of the East Ridge goal post. Only Coach Davis knew Coach Davis's system.

We had rushed for 175 yards to their 110, but we lost the game 12 to 7. It was bad enough to lose the game, but worst of all, we'd lost our coach.

The next day we found out that Davis was listed in fair condition. He'd be in the hospital for at least three weeks, with no timetable as to when we could expect him back on the sidelines. We asked if we could visit him and were told he could have no visitors for at least a week or two.

We were devastated with the loss of our leader, but we had to move on. We just had to focus on football and let God take care of the coach. The team would have to work hard and work together. Despite the loss to East Ridge, our season goals were still obtainable.

Chapter 47

Red Bank

Rock and roll was in the news.

Elvis Presley had been very popular in the late '50s, but had drifted off the map with the introduction of the music revolution of the '60s. Now trying to revive his career, he launched his first national tour since 1958; he was set to play in Phoenix at the Veterans Memorial Coliseum. Another rock star made the news. Jimi Hendrix, who was one of the headliners at Woodstock the year before, died of a drug overdose in London at the age of 27. At the time of his death, he was regarded as one of the best electric guitar players in the world.

Miss Walker was the oldest teacher in the English department. When talking about her age, Spook McKelvy, who had her for homeroom and English, would say, "She's so old, she was a waitress at the Last Supper."

Miss Walker loved Shakespeare. Her favorite was *Macbeth*. When she read this play, which she did often, it appeared she would go into a trance and visualize herself being on stage in an English theater. As she read aloud, she held the book in one hand and put her other hand near her mouth. She flicked her fingers up and down as she emphasized words while she read:

"To-morrow, and to-morrow, and to-morrow,
Creeps in this petty pace from day to day,
To the last syllable of recorded time;
And all our yesterdays have lighted fools
The way to dusty death…"

Her recital struck a chord with the football players. Coach Davis remained in the hospital, now in satisfactory condition.

Visitation was limited to family, so the only reports we got about his condition came from the coaches. Coach Catron was now the offense's coach and Coach Guedron handled the defense. Coach Smith helped out with both, but now also oversaw the Junior Varsity.

After Monday's practice, David Soloff came up to me as we walked up the hill and said he had me a date for Saturday night. I said, "What do you mean, you have me a date?"

He said, "There are these two sophomore girls who want to go out with us." He told me who they were.

I didn't know them, but I'd seen them and I had to admit they were cute. I thought, "Oh, a benefit of being a football star." Though I knew Cindy would be pissed off, I rationalized that we weren't officially going steady or anything like that. So it would be okay to go out with them; after all, I was just accommodating my buddy Soloff. I told him I'd go with him.

Our next game was at Red Bank. Although Red Bank was less than 10 miles from our campus, the two teams hadn't played each other since 1965. The Lion's Den, as their field was called, was rumored to be a tough place, in part due to the rabid fans and its reputation of getting favorable calls on close plays.

The kickoff was scheduled for 8 o'clock Friday night. We went through our normal preparations, got on the bus, and headed for Red Bank. Several of our guys knew some of their players. A couple of the Red Bank players went to North Chattanooga Church of God, where Eddie Roberson's father was the pastor. Alan Ridge, one of the Lion stars, had gone to church there since he was a small boy and was one of Eddie's good friends.

At the midfield coin flip, Bill Wilder went out to meet the refs and their captains, one of whom was Mike Ducker, who was one of Bill's teammates in junior high.

It was once again a sellout crowd with wall-to-wall people all around the stadium. It was estimated to be well over 7,000 people in attendance.

The game got under way. We fumbled the ball early in the first quarter on our 20-yard line and it was recovered by Red Bank's Casey Jones. Four plays later, Baggett, the Red Lion quarterback, ran in from the one-yard line for the touchdown. The extra-point kick was wide right. So the Lions took an early lead, 6 to 0.

The kickoff was fairly deep. I fielded the ball about the 10-yard line. The return was set up to run to the right, but as I headed that way, I saw that there were no openings. I cut back to the left and weaved my way up the field. As I crossed the 50-yard line, I could see only one defender ahead. He had the angle on me, but I thought I might outrun him to the goal line. As I reached the 10-yard line, he knocked me out of bounds.

The City High stands went crazy! We had the ball inside the Red Bank 10-yard line.

But there was a flag at a midfield. Oh no! The refs called clipping on Tommy Richmond. Our fans started booing in protest, but to no avail. The refs marched the ball back to our 47-yard line. (The next week when we reviewed the films, it was obvious that Tommy's block was clean and legal; it was clearly not a clip.) We scored anyway on a 10-yard run by Eddie Roberson. We missed the extra point, but had tied the game at 6.

Just before halftime, we got another break. It was fourth down and they were punting to us. The punter dropped the snap from center and we recovered the ball on the Lion 19. On the first play from scrimmage, Bill Wilder ran a naked bootleg around the left side for the touchdown. As we celebrated the score, lying on the field at the 16 yard line was our number 60. Tommy Richmond had been knocked out cold. The linemen gathered around him as Coach Catron and Coach Smith came on to the field. Coach Smith broke an ammonia cap and placed it under Tommy's nose, and he came to. He was helped off the field. Once Richmond was off the field, we lined up for the extra point. We missed it again, but took a 12 to 6 lead.

Tommy was now sitting on the bench with a glazed look on his face. One of the water boys gave him a cold towel to put around his neck.

Coach Smith asked him, "Are you seeing stars? Does your head hurt?"

Tommy shook his head no to both questions.

Then the coach held up two fingers and asked, "How many finger am I holding up?"

Tommy paused and stuttered out, "Two."

Then the big coach asked him, "What's your name? What's your phone number?"

Tommy answered both questions.

I don't know how Smith knew Richmond's phone number off the top of his head to know if Tommy was correct or not. I guess it sounded right. Anyway, he had passed the concussion test and Coach Smith declared him good to go in the second half.

Our lead didn't last long. After our kickoff, the Lions connected on a deep pass down to our 10-yard line, then scored two plays later. Their kick was good so we went to halftime behind 13 to 12.

As we headed to the locker room, Tommy remained on the bench looking at the ground. Lee Abelson, who was almost halfway to the locker room, saw Tommy still sitting on the bench. He went back and helped him up, then led him to the locker room. I guess Lee felt like he owed that to Tommy from the Jamboree game when he himself had been knocked out.

Richmond was back on the field when we got the ball early in the third quarter. Both teams traded punts back and forth with no scoring in the quarter.

At the midway point in the fourth quarter, we drove the ball 80 yards and scored on a one-yard quarterback sneak by Bill. This time we tried to run for the conversion, but we were stopped and the score stood at 18 to 13. We had the lead with four minutes to go in the game. We liked our chances; Red Bank hadn't been able to move the ball on us in the second half.

We kicked off and stopped them inside their 20-yard line. They would have to drive the ball almost the length of the field to win the game. They started the drive running the ball with a couple of good gainers. On third down, we knocked down a pass, but wouldn't you know it, a penalty flag was thrown. The ref called a pass-interference penalty on Denny Cornett, which gave them 15 yards and a first down. Of course, it sure didn't look like a penalty to us!

As time ticked down under two minutes, Baggett ran a bootleg for about 15 yards. The next play was a pass to Rose on a down-and-out route on my side. Baggett threw the ball and I broke in front of Rose, intercepted the ball, and fell to the ground. Rose jumped on top of me and tried unsuccessfully to wrestle the ball away from me. However, the referee nearest the play ruled that Rose had possession and gave them the ball on the three-yard line. I was so mad, I could have chewed a nail into dust, but it was their ball. Two plays later, they ran the ball in for their third touchdown. The extra point failed, but they had the lead, 19 to 18.

They kicked off to us with less than 40 seconds left in the game. We returned the kick to our 35-yard line. We had 65 yards to go and we hadn't thrown the ball the entire game. Our best bet was to run. We ran a couple of plays and got a first down, but now we had time for only one more play. The play came in from the sideline; it was a power sweep to Eddie.

Bill pitched the ball to Eddie; a convoy of maroon helmets led him around the right end. He got five yards, then ten yards, then Eddie broke out of the pack, with one guy to beat to the end zone. As Eddie neared the goal line, the entire stadium was standing and screaming. A lone blue-shirted Lion defender had the angle on him. Just when it looked like Eddie was past the lonely Lion and headed to the end zone, the defender dove toward Eddie and caught just enough of Eddie's leg to cause him to lose his balance and hit the ground at the 17-yard line. As Roberson was going down, the stadium horn sounded, ending the game. Eddie raised his head and looked back at the Lion defender who had stopped him; it was his childhood friend, Alan Ridge.

We had lost another game. We all felt that the referees had taken it away from us with those questionable calls. We now knew why the Lion's Den was a tough place to play: a big dose of home cooking! We'd hoped to give our sick coach good news, but it was not to be. A disappointed group of football players loaded on the bus.

On Saturday, Soloff picked me up and we went to fetch the sophomore girls, then headed up to Signal Mountain. David told me were going to a party at the house of friend of his who went to Baylor. He said his name was Garrett Strang.

I said, "You're kidding! I've known him since we were five years old. Garrett and I went to elementary school together for a couple of years."

Garrett played football at Baylor for Red Etter. Garrett's family had a house on the mountain in a section called Summertown. When we got to the party, Garrett and I greeted each other and spent a good while catching up, since it had been a couple of years since we'd seen each other. Our dates spent a lot of time smiling and giggling. I guessed that come Monday, they'd happily tell their friends that they'd been out with a couple of football players over the weekend. As for me, I'd have had a much better time if I'd gone out with Cindy.

For our next game, we were going to middle Tennessee to play Lawrenceburg. We hoped to break our losing streak.

Chapter 48

On the Road

Mike O'Neil was out of school after third period. This meant he could leave the campus without a special pass. Normally, Coach Catron was stationed at the entrance to the campus to check people coming and going. Since O'Neil had a free pass, he could drive by Catron and just wave to him as he left. So for lunch, he often took a couple of us with him. The lunch runs were worth the risk getting caught, so you could avoid having to eat cafeteria food. If you got caught leaving school without permission, it cost you ten detentions.

Cindy and I went with him on occasion to Hixson Pike to either the Pizza Hut or the Daily Queen. We just had to hide as O'Neil drove past Catron exiting the school parking lot. We had two options: We could lie on the back floorboard of his car or get in the trunk. Coming back was a little more of a challenge; the coach generally stopped the cars as they entered the campus parking lot. This meant that he might see you if you were on the floorboard. So the trunk was the only option. Well, after her experience with Sammye in the Mustang, Cindy still had an aversion to the trunk. She preferred a third option: climbing the fence.

The fence entrance was a little tricky. O'Neil drove into the neighborhood next to the school and dropped us off in front of David Jones's house, which backed up to school property. We walked through David's backyard and climbed the five-foot chain-link fence. Cindy would rather climb a fence than get in the trunk of another car.

Monday was a normal practice day. We started off watching

the film of the Red Bank game. We were all pretty dejected after the game and the calls we got. The film just made things worse. At the end of the viewing, Bill Wilder stood up and said, "Guys, we can't do anything about what happened Friday night. We just have to be committed to work even harder. Come on! Let's stay focused on getting better. We can still reach our goals for the year!"

We watched the film of Lawrenceburg's recent Friday game, then went to the upper field in shorts, shoulder pads, and helmets. After finishing our warm-ups, we worked on passing routes. I'm not sure why we did this; we didn't throw one pass in the Red Bank game. Okay, maybe we did need practice on our passing.

The backs and ends took turns running routes. It was my turn to run a pattern and Bill was throwing. I ran a down and out and he threw the ball a little out of my reach. I tried to sprint after it, but since I was watching the ball, I didn't see the concrete poles lying on the ground. Apparently, workmen had been repairing the fence and had left some poles, which had concrete around the bases, stacked up on the side of the field. With my eye on the ball, my right knee hit the concrete and I went down like a ton of bricks.

I thought for sure I'd broken my leg.

The coaches came running over and told me to take it easy. After a few minutes, I got up and limped off the field. I couldn't put any weight on my knee. I was told—what else?—to go see Dr. Dodds. He examined my knee and determined there were no breaks or ligament damage. It was only bruised. He said it would be swollen a couple more days, but to take aspirin and put ice on it at night, and I should be able to play on Friday.

I was held out of practice on Tuesday and Wednesday, but went back on Thursday with a special pad for my knee. Still, I could run at only about 70% speed. Since speed was part of my game, I knew it be would be a difficult night on Friday.

Friday we got out of school at 11, went to the locker room to pack our gear, and boarded a Greyhound bus for the 180-mile ride to Lawrenceburg, Tennessee. We had no idea where it was, but we found out it was the county seat of Lawrence County and a farming community with a population of about 9,000, located in the southern portion of middle Tennessee just north of the border of Mississippi and Alabama. Its real claim to fame was that Davy Crockett had lived there for a couple of years in the 1800s. Lawrenceburg was the only high school in the entire county. How Coach Davis found these guys to play was a mystery to us. But as we rolled out of the locker room to do warm-ups before the game, we noticed that once again we'd be playing in front of a packed house. It looked like everyone in the county was there. After all, what else was there to do in Lawrenceburg on Friday night? We were used to playing in front of big crowds, except this time, there weren't many Dynamo supporters. Only a few parents and our cheerleaders had made the trip.

Coach Catron told me that I'd be starting in my normal spots, despite the fact that my speed was down by around 30%.

After we traded the ball back and forth in the first quarter, we began to move the ball on the ground. We ended a 60-yard drive on a short run by Eddie Roberson, but missed the extra-point kick. So we led 6 to 0.

Lawrenceburg didn't look all that good, but they had one player, a black kid, number 89, who was all over the field. He was a good-size kid and was pretty quick. It seemed over the course of the game, he lined up in every position. He played linebacker, safety, or end on defense. On offense he lined up at halfback, fullback, and end. He also ran back the kickoffs and punts. He was clearly their do-everything guy.

By the time the second quarter started, we figured out that wherever 89 went, that was where the play was going. He either ran the ball or blocked for the ball carrier. They scored on a 30-yard pass play, but they also missed the kick and at the halftime break, it was tied at 6.

We kicked off to them to start the second half. Tommy Richmond lined up on the same side of the field as 89. He decided that he was going to take care of 89 once and for all. Tommy told himself that whether or not 89 ran the ball or was blocking, Tommy was unleashing a can of "whupp-ass" on him. Tommy said to himself, "The big guy is going down!"

The ball was kicked, with number 89 blocking. Tommy tore down the field like a missile fixed on his target. However, the closer Tommy got to 89, the bigger he looked. This caused Richmond to have second thoughts about his mission. At about 10 yards from this big guy, Tommy pulled up and side-stepped the big blocker, intending to call him a son of a bitch as he brushed by 89. But 89 never slowed down and headed right toward Tommy. He mowed over Richmond like a train hitting a groundhog. As he ran over Tommy, 89 kicked him in the head and muttered, "Take that, you son of a bitch. By the way, the name's Jackie Davis!"

About midway through the third quarter, we ground out a drive and David Sanders scored on a three-yard run. John Swanson scored the two-point conversion on a dive play. We took the lead 14 to 6. We held them for the remainder of the third quarter and halfway through the fourth quarter, and it looked like we'd get our first win.

We punted to them. It was a short punt. They got the ball in good field position with less than four minutes to go in the game. We just had to keep them out of the end zone. Unfortunately for the boys in maroon, we weren't able to do that.

Lawrenceburg started to move the ball and the drive was capped off as their do-it-all halfback, Jackie Davis, took off on a 19-yard run around the end for a touchdown.

The score was 14 to 12. Okay, now all we had to do was keep them from converting the two-point play. They lined up for two and we stacked the line in front of 89. But somehow or another, Davis managed to bust through our line and score the two-point conversion. The game was tied 14 to 14. We got the ball with less than a minute to go, but time ran out. We didn't lose, but we didn't win either. To those in the maroon helmets, it felt like a loss.

We learned one thing about Lawrenceburg that night: Jackie Davis, number 89, could play football. If he kept playing like that, he would surpass Davy Crockett as the most famous resident of Lawrence County, Tennessee.

As we walked to the locker room, we overheard one of our loyal fans, who'd made the long trip to West Tennessee, talk about the game. The old gentleman had seen almost every City High football game since the big war. He told his buddy, "This is the best team we've had in years. They should be three and oh. They're just snake bit!"

No doubt, we *felt* snake bit. After three weeks into the season, the team that was supposed to be one of the best in Eastern Tennessee had yet to win a game and their leader was still in the hospital. It was a long bus ride back to Chattanooga. We began to wonder if we would accomplish our goals for the year.

The following week, it wouldn't get any easier. We had to play unbeaten Riverside at Brainerd High.

Chapter 49

The First Win

At lunch on Monday, Jon Exum sat down next to me and started asking me about the Lawrenceburg game. I gave him the highlights. He told me not to worry; we could still beat Central this year, because after three games they hadn't fared any better. They'd yet to win a game. Jon was always good at trying to bring out the bright side of a dim story.

Jon's family, the Exums, owned the afternoon *Chattanooga News Free Press*, which didn't hurt our public relations. Jon liked to hang out with the football players. He had a camera, so I guessed he was working on a career as a photographer. He generally had his camera with him, even during school. He sometimes shot pictures at the games or school events. Some of his game photos ended up in the paper. Jon and I had gotten to know each other during lunch period in the Commons. Jon was a funny guy and was always making wisecracks.

Jon also liked to talk about football. He'd attended our first two games and he commented on my play. He said how he liked my style. He knew I'd hurt my knee before the Lawrenceburg game, but I played anyway. He said, "You're a tough guy, aren't you? A real hot shot. I'm going to call you Broadway Buck." This wasn't an original name; it had come from Broadway Joe, the nickname the New York Jets quarterback, Joe Namath, had been given after appearing on the cover of *Sports Illustrated* in 1965.

Nevertheless, Jon kept calling me Broadway Buck, or just Broadway, at school and sure enough, later in the week, my picture was in the paper with the caption "Broadway Buck." From that point on, some of the sports writers used the name when describing my play in Saturday recap articles about our Friday night games. In the course of a year, I'd gone from Carlton to Buck to Broadway Buck. It seemed I was finally one of the boys.

Meanwhile, football was growing more popular by the week. The competing AFL and NFL pro football leagues finalized their merger before the start of the 1970 season. The two leagues merged into two conferences, the American and the National. It was also the first time the leagues played regular-season games against each other. Three NFL teams, the Colts, Browns, and Steelers, moved into the American to balance out the conferences.

Historically, pro games were played on Sundays, but the merger brought on a new concept. On Monday September 21, 1970, ABC broadcast a game between the Cleveland Browns and the New York Jets. The hometown Browns won the game 31 to 21 and Monday Night Football was born.

On Friday afternoon, we arrived at the normal time for the Riverside game. My locker was near Bill Wilder's and Eddie Roberson's. They claimed to be superstitious and they always wore the same socks, T-shirts, and jocks for every game. Of course, they washed them after every game. I thought, "Everybody knows that if you wash them, the mojo is gone." I kept my washing-out-the-mojo theory to myself, but I did point out to them that we were 0-2-1 so far this year and that they might want to change their luck by getting a new set of undergarments. They both looked at me with dazed looks on their faces. After a short pause Eddie said, "Well, if we don't win tonight, I'm burning my jock and I'm getting a whole new set of undies!"

Riverside, the all-black school, was 3 and 0, and we were yet to win a game. Our basketball team had stopped their winning streak earlier in the year and we'd beaten them in football for the past couple of years, so some Riverside fans believed this would be a revenge game. There was also some black and white tension in the air, but it wasn't as intense as it had been at the basketball game. Part of it had to do with the fans being separated by 50 yards of football field.

After watching the films of their game, we knew that we were facing a team unlike any other we'd faced before. This team loved to pass the football and relied on passing more than running. In our three previous games, our opponents had greatly favored the run, so it would be a real test for our defense, especially the backs.

It had been over a week since I'd bruised my knee. It was healed now and I was able to run at full speed. By looking at the film of Riverside's last game, I'd need all my speed to keep up with the Trojan receivers.

On Friday we boarded the bus and headed to Brainerd to play our first home game of the season. We played home games at Brainerd and Kirkman. The City High game programs were on sale. All the moms and dads of the players wanted to be sure they got a program. On page three was a message from Principal Jim Phifer: "On behalf of the 1970 Dynamo football team and coaching staff, I would like to welcome you. We are all saddened by the absence of Coach Davis this season and would like to dedicate all our victories to him. We hope to have him back with us very soon."

Earlier in the week, our captains Bill Wilder and Joe Burns were interviewed by the newspaper. Both of them predicted that we would go undefeated the remainder of the year. This was a bold statement, but everyone on the team believed that would happen.

As we warmed up before the game, the bands were booming, but the crowd was much smaller than the ones at the East Ridge and Red Bank games.

Of course, our offensive game plan was the same as always: run the ball.

In the first quarter, we got on the scoreboard fairly early with a nine-yard run by Eddie Roberson. Of course, the kick failed.

Riverside came out throwing the ball. Russell Logan, their quarterback, had a strong arm and was fairly accurate, but our defense was able to hold them back.

In the second quarter, Eddie broke the line on a well-executed trap play and sprinted 40 yards for the score to record his second touchdown of the night. This time we tried to run the ball for a two-point conversion, but it was unsuccessful.

In the next series of downs, Logan threw a pass that was intercepted by Jim Brown, one of our linebackers. We got the ball at midfield, but after two plays from scrimmage, we fumbled and Riverside recovered.

Logan had been throwing the ball mostly on the other side of the field and after two tries in that direction, he came out throwing a down and out route to the receiver on my side. I saw it coming, stepped in front of the receiver, and intercepted the ball. I was tackled after about a 12-yard return.

Our offense took over on the 37-yard line and we moved the ball down the field. The drive was capped off with a four-yard run by Eddie. It was his third score of the night. The extra-point kick missed as the half came to an end.

We headed to the locker room with an 18-point led. We could hear the drums of the Riverside band booming in rhythm as they marched on to the field. While their football wasn't always that good, their band was great. They played and marched in a style similar to that of the Grambling College band. Grambling was an all-black university in Louisiana. The Grambling band had gained national recognition over the years as it performed at many national parades and events.

The marching Trojans looked sharp in their all-royal-blue uniforms trimmed in yellow. The jackets had bright brass buttons on the chest and the cuffs. On their heads, they wore a blue eight-inch-tall pillbox-style hat with a six-inch yellow plume with a short black bill in front. The band was led by eight majorettes wearing blue-sequin costumes. The Drum Major, who led the musicians on the field, was decked out in an all-white uniform trimmed in blue with a big white English-guard-style hat and black shiny boots that went all the way up to his knees.

It was a big band that covered most of the field between the 30-yard lines. Once the entire band was in position, the drums stopped and there was a moment of silence. Then the Drum Major blew a whistle and the band came to life. It seemed like all hell broke loose. They played a fast tempo and marched in rhythm to the music. While they marched, they also moved their instruments from left to right and up and down at the same time. The Drum Major high-stepped to the pace of the music as he led the band around the field. The show went on for about 10 minutes without taking a break. Then, with the sound of the Drum Major whistle, the music stopped and the blue-uniformed entertainers marched off the field to the beat of the drums. They were wildly cheered by both sides as they exited.

Though I didn't see it this time, I'd seen it a number of times before, so I knew it had been a great show. Most people in the stands were exhausted just watching it. Of course, a number of the white people in the stands had never seen anything like it. Some might have been offended by the style, because it was a black band and a nontraditional performance, but down deep, I'm sure they enjoyed it. How could they not?

In the second half on defense, Riverside ran an eight-man line. They dared us to throw the ball. Without Coach Davis, we didn't throw the ball, so we were pretty well bottled up.

On their side, they continued to throw and finally scored in the fourth quarter on a 40-yard pass, but the extra-point try failed. It was too little too late. The victory was within reach as the Troop chimed in with one of their typical cheers, "Pork chop pork chop thick and greasy we've got a team that beat you easy." This was the first time the Troop had anything to cheer about since basketball season.

We held on to run out the clock and got our first win, 18 to 6. Riverside had thrown the ball 38 times, with 13 completions for 186 yards. We'd rushed the ball for over 200 yards with no passing yardage. Needless to say, the Dynamos faithful were ecstatic; hopefully, the snake-bite curse was over.

The Saturday morning headline read, "Eddie Roberson 'Recks' Riverside." He did score three touchdowns, but little did Eddie know that he'd soon pay for that headline.

My play was also mentioned in the paper: Broadway Buck Buchanan made a couple of key tackles and had intercepted a pass.

Next up on the schedule was our Homecoming game against the Tullahoma Wildcats. We didn't know much about these guys, but we sure hoped to keep on winning.

Chapter 50

Homecoming

Homecoming was always an exciting time at schools.

It gave alumni the opportunity to reconnect with their former high schools and relive the memories of their times there. It was also a special celebration for the school, because of the festivities. At halftime on Friday, the Homecoming Queen would be announced. Then on Saturday night was the Homecoming Dance.

Monday afternoon as we sat down in the Armory to review films, we got some encouraging news. Coach Davis had been released from the hospital and would be resting at home for the next couple of weeks. Loud cheers and yells of excitement rang throughout the locker room.

Then we got some more good news. Steakley was fully recovered from his broken collarbone and was cleared to play.

As we were getting seated before the films started, Pat Petty started giving Eddie Roberson hell about "the Roberson 'Recks' Riverside" headlines in the Saturday paper. Petty scolded him by saying, "I guess you did all that own your own! Looks like us linemen might as well've been sitting in the damn stands, 'cause you don't need us!" Joe Burns, Tommy, and Lee also chimed in. Coach Catron and Coach Smith just chuckled. This went on for about five minutes. Then the bantering stopped. But it wasn't forgotten.

Tuesday was always scrimmage day. After warm-ups, we divided sides and got ready for the first-team offense to match up against the second-team defense. On the second play, Bill handed the ball to Roberson for a dive play up the middle. The offensive line stood up without attempting to block. The defensive linemen and linebackers stormed through the unguarded holes and smothered Eddie for a loss.

A few more plays were run by the other backs. So it could have been that the first play was just a lack of focus.

Then Bill called a sweep play for Eddie. Once again, the offensive line allowed the defenders to blitz through the gaps toward number 22 and gang-tackle him for a 10-yard loss.

As the defense unpiled and Eddie staggered to his feet, Petty went over to him and asked, "Are you going to give the linemen credit next time?"

"You bet," replied Roberson.

The entire team and all three coaches laughed. In the future, we were sure that Eddie would give the linemen the credit due for their blocking efforts.

During the week, Eddie Roberson and Bill Wilder talked Coach Catron into adding motion plays to the offense. In reality, Eddie was the main advocate of this strategy. It seemed that Eddie was a big fan of the Kansas City Chiefs and loved the way they used motion, plays in which the offensive backs are in motion when the ball is snapped. So in Eddie's mind, if it was good for the Chiefs, it must be good for the Dynamos. He convinced the coaches that the motion element would help spice up our offense. To me, we needed the forward pass added to our offense, not a pro-style gimmick. Anyway, with Eddie's insistence, we began to work on plays using motion.

Unbeknownst to me, there was a tradition at City High School on the Thursday before the Homecoming game. The cheerleaders and some volunteers "rolled" the yards of select senior players with toilet paper. On Friday morning at the breakfast table, E. Blaine told me that I had a job on Saturday morning. I looked at him, puzzled. He'd given me a reprieve from Saturday chores during football season. Then he said, "Just go look out at the front yard." I got up from the table, walked to the front of the house, and looked out the window.

Streamers of white toilet paper hung from the two trees and covered most of the lawn. Someone had actually done a very good job, as far as rolling a yard went. Also, in the center of the yard next to the steps was a football-shaped sign on a wooden stick stuck in the ground. On the sign was my jersey number 20 with the words, "Good Luck, Buck." While I was flattered to be recognized by the cheerleaders, I wasn't looking forward to climbing the trees Saturday morning and retrieving the toilet paper.

I later found out that Cindy, Sammy, and Sheron Bunch were the culprits. Apparently, the girls had made a night of rolling yards and my yard was the last stop on the way back to Sammye's, where Cindy and Sheron spent the night.

The Homecoming court was set. Sally Fuston, Judy Alday, Kathy Huffaker, Susan Massey, Gigi Galbraith, and Sheron Bunch were the candidates for queen. They'd been nominated by the football team and approved by faculty and staff. Three of the girls dated football players, so one would have thought that Judy, Kathy, and Susan had the inside track.

The kickoff was at 8 o'clock at Brainerd High. Being a home game, we wore our all-maroon uniforms. Tullahoma, Tennessee, was a small town on top of Monteagle Mountain some 70 miles west of Chattanooga, just off I-24 on the way to Nashville. They came into the game with a record of 1 and 2. At kickoff there was a decent-sized crowd; however, it was a little smaller than the Riverside crowd the Friday night before.

My sister Betty and her friend Sandra were in town to attend the Plum Nelly Art Festival on Saturday. It was an annual event held on the backside of Lookout Mountain. They planned to be at the game on Friday night.

Cindy was an alternate cheerleader, so she was on the sidelines cheering. I gave her a smile as I headed on to the field for the kickoff.

As the game got started, it looked like a defensive battle, since neither offense moved the ball. However, the Tullahoma team had a good strong punter who kept us deep in our territory most of the night.

As the second quarter began, their punter boomed another ball deep. I fielded it inside the five and got the ball out to the 10-yard line before I was gang-tackled. In three plays, we moved to the 26-yard line. Then we got a break in a trap play to the right. With two crushing blocks by Joe Burns and Pat Petty, Eddie Roberson broke the line, cut to the left, then sprinted 74 yards down the sideline for a touchdown. Ronnie Stinnett kicked the extra point, our first kicked extra point since the East Ridge game. We took a 7 to 0 lead into halftime.

As we headed to the locker room, I paused to watch as the City band, majorettes, and drill team marched onto the field. The band faced the home crowd and formed a semi-circle at the 50-yard line. The drill team split up and flanked the band on both sides. The majorettes positioned themselves in front of the band. Then Principal Phifer strolled out from the stands and stood in front of the majorettes.

From the north end, a parade of convertibles entered the field and drove around the outer perimeter. Each one of the girls on the Homecoming Court sat on top of the back seat in her own car as a driver drove them slowly around the field. The girls waved to the cheering crowd as they rode by. Once the cars had made a complete lap, they stopped in front of the home side, whereupon the girls got out of the cars and were escorted to the center of the field. The Press Box announcer called out over the stadium's PA system each girl's name and gave a brief description of the grade she was in and her school activities.

The drummers began a drum roll.

The announcement was made, ending the drama. Sheron Bunch was the 1970 City High School Homecoming Queen.

Of course, all of us football players knew she was the winner, because we'd voted for her.

Coach Phifer placed the crown on her head and she was handed a dozen red roses. With tears of joy running down her cheeks, she was all smiles as she waved to the crowd while walking to the car. She got in and started the slow victory lap around the field.

The Troop was seated on the right side of the student section. A few of the basketball players had joined the "football" Troop. Kenny Smith, Spook, and LeBron Crayton were now part of this special cheering group. As she rode passed the section of the stands where the Troop sat, they chanted, "Sheron! ..."

The second half continued to be a defensive struggle. Neither team moved the ball much. We even tried some of Eddie's motion plays, but they seemed to confuse us more than they did Tullahoma.

Lee Abelson was having a tough time of it. It seemed like he was getting beat by their defensive tackle on almost every play. Coach Smith even asked Lee if he was hurt. When his performance didn't improve, at the beginning of the fourth quarter, Coach Smith put big Vince Williams, the black kid I'd driven to practices, in the game. After a few plays, it looked like Vince had plugged the hole and Lee got the rest of the night off.

Pat Petty, while playing nose guard on defense, had battled all game with their center. The center probably outweighed him by 60 pounds, but Pat was much quicker and could get around him. This made the center mad. He was doing everything he could to stop Pat, even if it meant he had to hold, tackle, or trip Pat. It seemed like after every play there was pushing and shoving and they had to be separated.

The game went into the fourth quarter with us still holding on to the seven-point lead. So far we'd held their running game to 30 yards. So on the next series of downs, Tullahoma started throwing the ball. They were now passing on every down. They completed only four passes in the game, for short gains. The four times they had the ball in the fourth quarter, it was three plays and punt.

They got the ball back at midfield with less than two minutes remaining in the game. Once again they tried a pass, but this time John Swanson intercepted it at our 30-yard line and zigzagged his way to the Wildcat 40. Two plays later, the game ended and we'd won our second game in a row.

As usual we went to midfield to shake hands with the opposing team. All of a sudden, Pat Petty and their center started yelling at each other, then pushing, and then—you guessed it—a fight broke out. Some tried to separated Pat and the other guy, but then other fights broke out. Now there was pushing, shoving, and swinging helmets all over the field. I was always told when a fight breaks out, keep your helmet on, so my helmet stayed on my head. The coaches finally stopped the fight, but they kept us on the field until all the Wildcats were in the visitor's locker room. Then we headed to the bus. Leave it to Petty to start a fight when we were supposed to show good sportsmanship by shaking hands after a game.

After five games, our cross-town rivals, Central, had yet to win one. Joe Lee Dunn's boys were having a tough time scoring.

They finally scored two touchdowns in a game, but lost to Brain-erd 14 to 13.

We, on the other hand, were beginning to feel pretty good about our team. We'd added another win to our record and the Homecoming Dance was the next night.

Chapter 51

The Homecoming Dance

During the Tullahoma game, I lost a contact lens. So I played part of the game with one eye. This wasn't anything new; I'd lost seven of them so far this year. It seemed like once a week I was going to the optometrist to get a replacement. When I got to the Armory after the game, I took out the remaining contact and wrapped it up in athletic tape, because I didn't have a contact case. I wore my glasses to a party on the mountain. When I got home, I put my contact, wrapped in athletic tape, on the kitchen table.

When I got up the next morning, it was nowhere to be found. My mother had no idea where it was. Then my sister told me she'd had thrown it in the trash. She said, "It just looked like an old piece of white tape."

Of course, by the time I got up that morning, E. Blaine had already put the kitchen trash outside in the big trash can. So for the next 30 minutes, I got to sift through the trash looking for my contact, until lo and behold, I finally found it.

After retrieving my contact, I ate breakfast and commenced to cleaning up the toilet paper in the front yard. I mainly had to work on getting it out of the trees. Using a ladder and climbing out on the branches, I retrieved most of it without falling and breaking my neck. My dad did me a favor by picking up it up off the ground. I hoped I wasn't this popular in the future.

On the other side of Brainerd Road, Lee Abelson was doing a self-evaluation as to why he'd had such a bad game. He concluded that he was looking forward to a date he'd made for after the game and, therefore, wasn't as focused as he should've been. So right then and there, he decided to become an only-Saturday-night-date guy. Fridays were reserved for football and football only.

But now he was faced with what to do after the game, when everyone else was going out. Well, he was always hungry after playing four quarters of football. Since he was a non-working high-school kid with limited funds, he figured he could stop off at the Krystal, get 20 hamburgers, two fries, and a large Coke to go, then watch "Shock Theater" on his TV. He was convinced that this ritual would allow him to focus on football and there would be no more crappy games from the left tackle.

The Homecoming Dance was the biggest dance of the fall semester. Most of the guys on the football team had dates. Bill Wilder took Kathy Huffaker, Randy C. Gray went with Susan Massey. Of course, Sammye and Kenny went together. Spook and Marc double-dated; Marc took Gigi and Spook took Zenda Hall. Cindy and I met Tommy and Patty at the Town and Country for a pre-dance dinner. Mike O'Neil and Eileen Dooley joined us; it was their first date. As usual, a bunch of other City kids were in the restaurant. Tommy and I followed the normal script, ordering hamburgers, while the girls got steaks.

After dinner, we headed to the high school. There, we met another group in the parking lot. Mike Pendergrass and Janis Miles were sitting in his car drinking rum Icees. Pendergrass had gone to Northside Junior High, but was now going to Baylor. This was the first time I'd met him, but most everyone else knew him, because he'd gone to school with them before high school.

Mike played football at Baylor, where Red Etter was now coaching. It was Etter's first year at the all-boys school after moving over from Central High, so I asked him how it was playing for the famous coach.

Mike said, "When it was announced that Etter was coming to Baylor, all the returning players were scared as to what to expect. After all, he was a legend. We were surprised to find out it was a big change from the previous coach, but not what we expected. Coach Etter is a cerebral coach with a calming demeanor. He spends his time studying film and developing a game strategy and lets his assistants run the practices. He does demand perfection when it comes to running the plays. And he makes us think about football as a game of strategy, rather than a game of brute strength."

We had to be a little more careful this year with our drinking before a dance. Don Smith, the Spanish teacher who didn't care if you were drinking or not, was no longer teaching at the school. He suddenly left City last year near the end of the second semester, due to some personal problems. We knew Ms. Prior was guarding the main entrance, but we weren't sure who was manning the second door. Well, we got into the dance with no trouble.

As usual, there was a good crowd. The band was playing and a few kids were dancing, but it would take a while for everyone to get up and out on the floor.

To my surprise, Eddie Roberson was there. See, Eddie went to the Church of God and their church doctrine prohibited dancing. I told him it was good to see him. He said, "You know, I love to dance and I just couldn't resist the opportunity to celebrate our Homecoming victory. Please don't say anything about me being here if you see my dad around the school."

I knew his father, the Reverend Marshall Roberson. "Eddie, your secret's safe with me."

About midway through the dance, the music stopped and the Homecoming Queen and her court were introduced. Once again, Sheron Bunch had a big smile on her face as she was presented to the student body. The dance went on until eleven. Then we all went our own ways.

Cindy and I took off to her house; she had to get up early for a church program the next morning. Marc and Spook took their dates for a tour of the parking lot at the Chickamauga Dam. The dam parking lot was a great place to go at the end of date night to look for submarines in the Tennessee River. After a minute or two of searching in vain for periscopes, you had to find something else to do—sitting in a car in the dark isolated parking area.

Coach Davis had been released from the hospital earlier in the week and we'd be allowed to visit him next week. We hadn't seen him in four weeks, so we were all looking forward to the visit.

Chapter 52

A Win for the Coach

Coach Davis was resting at home. The doctor had put him on a restricted diet and told him to quit smoking and not get excited, but he could watch game film.

A few of the other guys had been to see him on Monday. Tommy Richmond, Mike O'Neil, and I went by after the Tuesday practice. Although he'd lost weight, he looked good and was in good spirits. He said he'd already started watching film. He talked about what plays should have been called in the East Ridge game that could have easily led to a couple of scores. He'd also reviewed the Red Bank game and said there was no doubt some bad calls cost us the game. "I can't wait to get back," he said. "The hardest part about being in the hospital was not being on the field with you guys."

We asked him when he expected to be back.

He said, "If everything looks good at my doctor visit at the end of the week, I'll be back at school next week."

We didn't stay long, but we did promise him that we would beat Tyner this coming Friday.

He replied, "Good. If we let them beat us, their coach will give me a hard time for the rest of the year." Tyner High was where Davis had coached before coming to City; the team was led by an outstanding running back, Mike DeRossett.

The Tuesday paper gave a rundown of the game. In the article, Eddie Roberson was quoted as saying: "Listen, you write this down. I want Tyner and Mike DeRossett so bad I can taste it. Don't tell me how tough they are!" Well, if the 4-and-1 Tyner Rams team didn't have enough motivation before, they sure as hell had plenty now, thanks to Eddie's big mouth. DeRossett had been out several games with an ankle injury, but the buzz was that he was expected to play Friday.

The Tyner team was almost a mirror image of ours. They ran a similar offense and the same defense as the Dynamos. Although now that Eddie Steakley was cleared to play, we might throw the ball a little.

On Friday, we boarded the yellow school bus and headed to the other side of the county. As we were walking to the locker room, we saw signs around the field about how the Rams planned to destroy the Dynamos. A few simply read, "Kill Roberson!"

We received the ball on the opening kickoff, but neither team did much on offense to start. As soon as the Rams got the ball the first time, we saw that their heralded tailback DeRossett wasn't in the game. Apparently, his hurt ankle would not allow him to play.

At the start of the second quarter, Eddie Roberson, playing safety, picked up a fumble on Tyner's 38-yard line and we started to move the ball. Our offense mainly used running plays, but believe it or not, we did throw one pass. We scored with less than four minutes in the first half. Naturally, we missed the extra point and were up 6 to 0.

Tyner took the kickoff and ran it back to their own 31-yard line, but our defense stood strong and actually pushed them back to the 26, where they tried a halfback option pass. Deflected by Joe Burns,it was intercepted by our defensive end, Mike O'Neil, who ran the ball back for the score. Ronnie Stinnett kicked the extra point and we led at halftime 13 to 0.

Neither team scored in the third quarter. With less than five minutes to go in the game, Tyner finally scored a touchdown, but they missed the extra point. When the final whistle blew, we'd held on for a 13-to-6 victory.

It had been a very hard-fought game. Fortunately for us, we didn't have any major injuries; however, the talented Tyner team suffered three injuries during the contest. What was even more interesting was that we finally had a passing game. Wilder threw for 75 yards, while on the ground we rushed for just over 100. There was no telling what we could do with a passing attack!

Saturday morning, Arch Trimble's mother called me and told me that Arch got hurt in his game the night before. His spleen had ruptured while he was making a play. He was in the hospital, would be there for a couple of days, and most likely would come home for a couple of weeks to recover. Unfortunately for him, his football days were over.

That night there was a party at Sally Fuston's house on Signal Mountain. Her parents were out of town, leaving her brothers in charge. They were only a couple of years older than Sally and they were nowhere in sight. So it was a normal high-school party, though unsupervised. The stereo was blasting and there were snacks and Cokes. Oh yes, some kids brought beer or some form of liquor to mix with the Cokes. The normal crew of boys and girls from City were there, along with Freddy White, Sally's boyfriend from McCallie. Freddy and I spent a good deal of time talking about football.

Suddenly, we heard a commotion coming from outside. Freddy and I ran outside to find a fight going on in the street in front of Sally's house.

I wasn't surprised that it involved Eddie Steakley. A young sophomore, who'd had too much to drink but was about half of Steakley's size, had been joking with Eddie and got sucker punched. Blood was pouring out of the young kid's nose and Steakley had the boy's head between the door jam and the front door of Steakley's car. Steakley was pressing the door on the kid's head—like putting the kid's head in a vise. I thought Steakley was going to kill the kid. Fortunately, Marvin Day pulled Steakley him off the kid and some other boys dragged the victim out of harm's way. One thing remained clear: If Eddie Steakley showed up at a party, trouble wasn't far behind. He was just a mean son of a bitch!

The headline the next morning in the *Chattanooga Times* was: "City's Awakening Giant at Last." Sportswriter Walt Howell's story was about how the Dynamos were finally living up to their pre-season billing after being mistreated by Lady Luck.

Coach Davis had been cleared by the doctors to return to school on Monday. So we looked forward to more success in the weeks to come.

Chapter 53

Davis Returns

We were all glad to see Coach Davis and our level of confidence got a big boost.

Just after third period, an announcement came over the PA system for Bill Wilder and Eddie Roberson to report to the Armory. When they got there, the Coach told them to come into his office and he closed the door. The serious look on Davis's indicated that this wasn't a welcome-back-to-school party.

He said, "Tell me something. Whose idea was it to use motion plays during the games?"

Bill looked at Eddie and said, "It was Eddie's idea."

"We aren't the Kansas City Chiefs. Our offense has never included any motion plays and it still doesn't! Do you understand that?" After hammering home his point for what seemed like another 15 minutes, he took a sip of his heart medicine and told the boys to leave. Welcome back, Coach Davis!

The 1970 World Series ended with Baltimore rebounding from the previous year's embarrassing loss to the Mets by beating the Cincinnati Reds in five games. Sparky Anderson's Big Ma-chine was led by Johnny Bench and Pete Rose, but they were no match for the Birds from Maryland.

Kirkman was our next foe that Friday. Their record was 3-and-3. The Golden Hawks were a big team. Gee, they must have outweighed us by at least 40 pounds a man. Their line was anchored by Gary Shinall, who weighed over 300 pounds, and he was flanked by Johnny Goodman and Wayne Turner, both well over 240 pounds. Their tailback Billy Joe Matthews went about 230. Billy Joe had already scored 42 points so far the season, which put him as one of the leaders in the county. The year before, we'd beaten Kirkman 53 to 0. But this year, the Hawks were a much better team. They were confident that they could revenge last year's embarrassment.

With Coach Davis back on the sidelines, we felt we had the upper hand despite the size difference. We believed our speed would be the difference in the game. Our game plan was to run straight at them in the beginning, then shift to trap plays as the game progressed.

The game was played at Kirkman's field, which sat up in the corner of downtown Chattanooga on Cameron Hill overlooking the Tennessee River. For a mid-October night, it was cold. There was a good crowd, all wrapped up in warm clothing.

As we lined up on the field to receive the kickoff, it was a good feeling to see Coach Davis standing there in his maroon jacket. It had been six weeks since the East Ridge game where he'd suffered his heart attack during halftime. He looked good, although he did have his heart medicine in his pocket and Dr. Dodds was standing next to him, just to be on the safe side.

For most of the first quarter, both teams slugged it out without making much progress. But with less than three minutes remaining in the quarter, things began to change. On fourth and seven from our 15-yard line, our punter, Denny Cornett, was set up to receive the snap from center. The ball sailed over his head. Denny scooped it up in our end zone, avoided a few would-be tacklers, and was brought down on our six-yard line. Three plays later, Billy Joe Matthews broke through the line and scored. They missed the extra point, but the Hawks were up 6-to-0.

As we jogged to the sidelines, Pat Petty turned to me and said, "If we lose this game, I'm going to whip your ass." I didn't say anything to him. I was nowhere near the scoring play, so I had no idea what he was talking about. Nonetheless, that was Pat. I later found out that he also threatened several of the guys on the team.

Pat didn't wait too long to ease his frustrations. On the ensuing kickoff, David Sanders fielded the ball on the left side and wove his way down the field to the Hawk's 24. Early in the second quarter, we worked the ball down to the nine-yard. On fourth and nine, rather than try a field goal, we opted for a pass play. Steakley ran a post pattern and Bill hit him in the hands for our first score of the night. Ronnie Stinnett kicked the extra point and with only 18 seconds gone in the quarter, we were ahead 7-to-6.

On the next set of downs, we stopped them in three plays. Eddie Roberson and I were back to receive the punt in a double-safety formation. In this formation, the safety who doesn't field the ball moves in front to lead the blocking on the return. As I fielded the punt, I looked up and the entire right side was open, with a straight path to the goal line. I knew that from Eddie's position, he also saw the opening.

I started to run with the ball and Eddie turned to me and yelled, "Run, Buck! Run!"

I appreciated his cheer. The only problem was that he was the only guy who could block the Kirkman end sprinting down the field on the left, coming straight at me from my blind side. But Eddie was so busy cheering me on, the Kirkman defender ran right past him and hit me about chest high. A hard tackle, it knocked the wind out of me. I lay on the ground trying to catch my breath thinking, "If only Eddie had blocked that guy, I would have scored."

Eddie helped me up and said, "Sorry, Buck. I should have hit that guy."

I just looked at him as I walked slowly toward the sidelines.

When the second-quarter whistle blew to end the half, we were holding onto the 7-to-6 lead. In the chill of the night, the bands and drill teams hit the field, while we warmed up and listened to Coach Davis in the locker room.

In the third quarter, we traded the ball back and forth. With about two minutes to go, Davis called a trap play. Pat Petty dealt a crushing blind-side blow to the Kirkman defensive tackle. That sprung Eddie Roberson for a 58-yard scamper down the sidelines for a touchdown. Stinnett kicked the extra point and we extended our lead to 14-to-6.

We kicked off to them and they began to move the ball. On this set of downs, I would get my first real introduction to Mr. Matthews. I'd been in on a couple of gang tackles of Billy Joe, but I hadn't had a one-on-one experience with him yet. Well, on this play, his offensive line had cleared out a gaping hole in our defensive line. The Golden Hawks's leading scorer came charging through the hole. Our tackle and linebacker were nowhere to be found. I was the only one standing between him and the end zone. As he charged toward me, I didn't even think about the fact that he outweighed me by 75 pounds. I just knew I had to tackle him. I set my feet. I lowered my shoulder. I could see that he wasn't planning on running around me, but intended to run over me. So just before he reached me, I thrust toward him and hit him at the knees. He slammed into me at what seemed like the speed—and the power—of a locomotive. He moved me back about three yards, but I managed to hold on to him and bring him down for a short gain. I lay on the ground for a few seconds and as I slowly got up, all I could see were stars and they weren't the ones in the sky. O'Neil helped me up and I went back to my cornerback position, shaking my head and getting ready for the next play. That was the hardest hit I'd taken so far in the season. Now that I'd made the acquaintance of Mr.

Matthews, I didn't really want to meet him again.

As we headed into the fourth quarter, we got some bad news. On the first offensive play of the final quarter, our fullback John Swanson limped off the field with a leg injury. Dr. Dodds looked at the leg. It was broken and John was out for the rest of the year.

We lined up to run the next play, one of our few tricks. We were in our normal "T" formation, Eddie Steakley at right end and Eddie Roberson the left halfback. The ball was snapped and Bill Wilder tossed it back to Roberson. It looked like a quick pitch run to the left. Roberson, who threw the ball with his left hand, ran about eight yards. Still behind the line of scrimmage, he raised up and threw the ball to Steakley, who had run a deep post pattern. Steakley caught the ball and bulled his way down to the three-yard line before two Hawk defenders stopped him.

Two plays later James Lawson, the fullback who replaced Swanson, went over for the score. James's running style was much different than Swanson's. John was a tough runner, but he had a little more finesse. Lawson, on the other hand, ran hard, low to the ground, and in a straight line. He was like a runaway bull and difficult to tackle. We missed the extra point.

We kept Kirkman bottled up the rest of the game, which ended with us on top 20-to-6.

At the final whistle, we all rushed over, picked up Coach Davis, put him on our shoulders, and carefully carried him to midfield to meet the Kirkman coach.

Things were back to normal. Our coach was back in action. As we headed off the field toward our sideline, head cheerleader Sheron Bunch came up to Coach Davis and planted a big kiss on his cheek. She told him how glad the school was to have him back.

A red-faced coach smiled and said, "It's good to be back!"

We all clapped and cheered!

Our record improved to 4-2--1. Next up were the Brainerd Rebels.

Central had finally begun to make some positive moves in their season. Over the previous two weeks, they'd tied Red Bank and stomped Notre Dame 48 to 8. They seemed to be hitting their stride as the annual clash with us was getting closer.

We didn't really care. We had our coach back and felt great about where we were headed.

Chapter 54

The Home of the Rebels

It had been quiet at Brainerd High so far this semester. There had been no reports of racial disturbances, as there had been the previous year. It appeared that the compromises made during the summer had solved the problems.

Going into the Brainerd game, most of the sports writers picked us to win. The two teams had played ever since Brainerd High School opened in 1961. But City had managed to win only two games during that time-frame. Coach Pete Potter had coached the Rebels from the beginning and he was still on the sidelines. Last year, his team had gone undefeated and ended up ranked number two in the state. While graduation had hit them fairly hard, they were still very tough.

The game was played at Brainerd's field. I'd gone to many Brainerd games over the years and was very familiar with the stadium and the Brainerd tradition. But as we took the field for warm-ups, I noticed something was different. No Confederate flags were flying, the band wasn't playing "Dixie," and there was no white horse with a student rider dressed as a Rebel soldier riding up and down the sidelines.

We wore our all-maroon uniforms and they were wearing their all-Carolina-blue uniforms with white helmets. No matter what the outcome, it would be a colorful game! But again, their helmets were missing something: the Confederate flag. I'd always thought the red and blue flag on the white headgear looked cool, but it had been removed. The stadium looked to be packed and it was reported to be a sold-out crowd.

Since I'd lived in this area of Chattanooga all of my life, except when I was away at Castle Heights, I knew several players on the Rebel team, either from elementary school, Dalewood Junior High School, or summer baseball. Greg Walton was a black kid and played end. I'd played football with him in the seventh grade at Dalewood. At that time, I considered Greg to be my first black friend who was my age. He was a good player and a good guy. I was sure we would meet during the contest.

As the game got underway, we took over early. Pat Petty recovered a fumble on the Brainerd 23 and two plays later, Eddie Roberson ran 13 yards for the score. The extra point was blocked, but we were up 6-to-0.

We kicked off to them and held them on three plays. I fair caught the punt on our 36. On the second play of the drive, Lee Abelson and Tommy Richmond cleared a path, allowing Roberson to scamper out of the backfield for a 61-yard score. This time, we tried a passing play for the conversion, but Bill Wilder's ball sailed over the head of our end Greg Daily. We had a 12-to-0 led with only seconds remaining in the first quarter.

The second quarter started with little movement by either team. At the eight-minute mark, Petty recovered another fumble. We had it first and 10 on the Brainerd 49. After one first down, Coach Davis called our trick play, the halfback pass. Eddie Roberson hit Steakley on this same play we'd run against Kirkman the week before. This time Steakley was brought down on the five-yard line. Two plays later, fullback James Lawson bulled his way over right guard for the touchdown. We tried another pass for the two-point conversion, but the pass was knocked down by the Brainerd defense.

We stopped Brainerd again and Mike Langley, the Rebel punter, boomed a 57-yard kick. David Sanders was back with me in the double-safety; Eddie Roberson's ankle was bothering him. Sanders called for the punt, but the ball fell through his hands and Brainerd recovered on the three-yard line. Two plays later, they scored over right tackle. The extra-point kick failed, so we went into halftime leading 18-to-6.

We moved the ball fairly well in the second half, though without scoring. We also held them for most of the half. As time ticked down to less than four minutes to go in the game, the Rebels got going. The Brainerd quarterback threw a long pass to wide receiver Greg Walton, my old friend.

I was covering Greg with the help of safety Gary Rundles. I went up for the ball and thought I had it intercepted, but Greg wrestled the ball away from me for the Rebel score. As we got up after the play, I said, "Nice play." He smiled at me and said, "You made it tough on me. I just got lucky." Their extra point failed.

With two minutes to go, they tried an onside kick, which Pat Petty recovered. The clock ran out and we secured an 18-to-12 victory.

As usual, we walked to middle of the field to shake hands with our opponents. I went up to Greg and talked to him for a few minutes. It was good to see him.

Our record was now 5-2-1 and with two games remaining, it look like our goals of having a better season than the previous year and beating Central were still obtainable.

The next day was the third Saturday in October, traditionally the day that the University of Tennessee played the Alabama Crimson Tide. The game was played in Knoxville. Scanning Bear Bryant's sideline, there wasn't one black face to be found. It was 1970, yet a black player had yet to wear the crimson and white of the University of Alabama. The Volunteers won the game by a score of 24-to-0.

Heck, our high schools had made more progress when it

came to some of the colleges. But our racial character would be tested the following week as we played the all-black Howard Tigers.

Chapter 55

The Tiger's Scorn

On my way from the Commons to the Armory for the Monday afternoon film session, I stopped in the bathroom near the auditorium. As I opened the door, I heard some commotion. I walked in and there was Eddie Steakley standing over Charles Gerber. They'd obviously been fighting. Charles, a sophomore who played on the football team, was the brother of John, whom Steakley had fought with during spring practice. I guess Steakley didn't like the Gerber family. Charles was as tough as his brother and wouldn't back down from a fight, even if he was outmatched. Charles's eye was swollen and his shirt was ripped.

It looked like Steakley was getting ready to kick Charles.

I said, "What's going on?"

Steakley turned around and replied, "This is another one of those damn Gerbers and I'm going to kick his ass!"

I looked Steakley in the eye, while bracing myself for his sucker punch, and said, "He's had enough! If you want to fight someone, you can fight me, but leave him alone!"

I'd been at the school a little over a year and so far had avoided a confrontation with this big bad-ass. Steakley didn't say a word, but he did turn red in the face. He looked down at Charles, then turned slowly back toward me and said, "Okay, that's enough." Turning, he walked out the door.

As I blew out a sigh of relief, I helped Charles up and he said, "Thanks." He cleaned up and I finished my original business and we headed to the Armory.

During the film session, Steakley acted like nothing had

happened. I really didn't want to fight him, but it was time that someone stood up for the little guys he liked to pick on. I didn't care for Steakley as a person, but when he was on the football field, he was part of the team.

We were gaining recognition in the region and the state as being a pretty good team. We were even getting votes to be included in the polls for the top 20 football teams in the state.

Our next game was with Howard, the oldest all-black school in the area, with its origins going back to the late 1800s. The school was named after Civil War Union General Oliver O. Howard.

Their record was 4-1-2. When it came to the black schools in Chattanooga, Howard always had the toughest football team. Riverside was known for its band and basketball teams, while Howard was known for being tough on the gridiron, regardless of their record.

We were the home team at Kirkman High School. The field was wet and muddy, since it had rained most of the day. It was also a cool damp night on top of that hill. We were once again clad in all maroon and Howard wore their white jerseys with maroon numbers, gold pants, and golden helmets with a maroon stripe down the middle flanked by white strips on either side. As they lined up on the sideline before the kickoff, they looked a lot bigger than we were. We knew it would be hard-hitting game.

It was another packed house. The mainly white City High fans sat on the home side with its back to the Tennessee River.

The first half was purely defense; neither team mustered much offense.

At the end of the first quarter, Roberson was gang tackled. He went down hard and was slow to get up. He'd hurt his ankle again and most likely wouldn't play rest of the game. I'd have to play most of the game in Eddie's position on offense, while still handling my regular duties on defense and kick returns.

They had a huge defensive end, Michael Scofield. I was assigned to block him, but with no success. When I tried to block him up high, he threw me out of the way. When I blocked him low, he ran over me. As the night wore on, I never got a good clean block on that guy.

We tried running the ball right at them, with no luck. All of our backs, including me, were getting creamed when we got the ball. A three-yard gain was considered successful. Also, winding up at the bottom of a pile of players after tackles was a dangerous place to be, with a lot of punching, biting, pinching, and pulling leg hairs. Of course, the refs didn't see this and there wasn't much you could do about it, other than yell. It was just part of an intense contest.

When David Sanders was at the bottom, as we unpiled, the Howard players would make cracks like, "How'd you like that, Uncle Tom?" referring to the 19th century novel about slavery in the South, in which and Uncle Tom was a slave who was faithful to his white master.

Despite the hard hits, we held them in check. The first half ended tied at 0. The second half was much of the same—all defense. I was on the field the whole time and it was the hardest-hitting game I'd ever played in. Maybe Roberson had the right idea about getting an ankle injury. Every play, they tried to knock your head off. Of course, we tried to do the same to their players.

The Tigers passed the ball some in the second half, but they had little success. It was still a scoreless game at the end of the third quarter.

At the start of the fourth quarter, we punted to Howard and they got the ball on their 42-yard line. They now concentrated on the running game. Calvin Stoudemire was their workhorse. On second and 10 at our 27-year line, they pitched the ball to Stottlemyre. He gained a couple of yards and it looked like we had him stopped at the 25, but he broke free and scampered final 25 yards for the game's first score. The two-point conversion run failed. As the clock ticked down to six minutes in the game, Howard held a 6-to-0 over the Dynamos.

With Eddie Robinson out of the game, we had to mount a game-winning drive without our star running back. I received the kickoff on about the 10-yard line and ran it back to the 23.

Coach Davis knew we needed to include some passing in the play selection in order to drive the 70-plus yards. With the game on the line, Steakley seemed to step up his intensity. He even began to throw some great blocks as we began our drive. Blocking was something that Steakley didn't normally do. But he was big enough to block their giant defensive end, Scofield.

After a couple of first downs, we were on the 50-yard line. As the clock continued running down, Wilder hit me with a screen pass in the right flat. Steakley made another great block and I ran 15 yards to near the 30-yard line. A 10-yard pass to Steakley got us down to the 21. After a short gain by Lawson, David Sanders was stopped for no gain. Then a third-down pass to Mike O'Neil fell short, but Howard was called for a roughing-the-quarterback penalty—our biggest break so far in the game.

The Howard coach, Lee Derek, went nuts. He argued that it not only wasn't a penalty, but it was a good clean hit on Wilder. He argued and argued with the head referee, to no avail. The penalty stayed as called. As the ref walked off the penalty, the Howard faithful let out a loud round of boos.

We had a first down on the 10-yard line. Two plays later, Wilder hit Steakley with a pass in the corner of the end zone for a touchdown. Steakley had used his basketball block-out move to get position on the defensive back and caught the pass like getting a rebound off the backboard. The game was tied 6-to-6.

Driving the ball 78 yards down the field, we'd completed five passes in the process. Amazing!

Now, with 50 seconds remaining on the game clock, we lined up to kick the extra point.

I was on the right side as a blocking back. The ball was snapped. Wilder put the ball down and Ronnie Stinnett kicked it. It sailed into the air. To me, it looked like the ball was wide to the right. I hung my head, thinking, "No way that kick is good."

Then I heard cheers. "Huh?"

I looked up to see that the referee had raised his arms high in the air, signaling that the extra point was good. I was shocked!

We had the lead, 7-to-6. As I walked to the sidelines after a brief celebration with my teammates, I was surprised that the Howard team didn't protest the call on the kick. I guess they were still mad over the roughing-the-passer penalty.

We won the game and were now 6-2-1. The City crowd was cheering with great jubilation, while the Howard crowd seemed madder than hell about the way the game had been officiated. Some of the Howard players refused to shake hands with us after the game. We loaded on the bus for the victory ride across the river.

The bus started to head down the driveway behind the visitors' stands through a large crowd of Howard fans who were yelling, booing, and cussing us. When it had to stop to wait on traffic, several Tiger fans began beating on the bus and rocking it back and forth. Just as the bus was about to tip over, the police arrived and the fans scattered. Then we got a police escort out of the stadium down to Broad Street.

The Howard game had been the toughest game I would play in all year. I came out of it with bruises, cuts, and aches all over my body. But there was good news, too. We had a week off before we closed out the season against our arch-rival, Chattanooga Central.

Chapter 54

The Off Week

We had hoped to get Monday off, since we had two weeks to prepare for the Pounders, but no such luck. Coach Davis stuck to our normal schedule—except this week, we would also have to practice on Friday.

The Tuesday after the Howard game, their coach continued to protest the way our game had been officiated. *The Chattanooga Times* wrote an article about the officiating, stating that it wasn't anything new for black teams. Howard, Riverside, and practically every Negro high school in the state had complained about the officiating in games with white schools ever since the two races began playing each other in football in Tennessee in 1965. It used to be that Howard was penalized as much as 150 yards in game when they played a white school, but today the officials weren't quite as blatant. Now they were only accused of calling the key penalties, like when the teams neared a goal line or a call might impact a scoring play. Coach Derek had showed the City vs. Howard film at the weekly Tuesday night officials' meeting. The officials admitted that the call might have been wrong, but it wasn't changed.

I thought the missed extra point was a bigger blown call than roughing the passer, but home cooking was nothing new for games in the South. We felt like we would've won the Red Bank game if not for the excessive penalties called against us. So in some cases, home cooking wasn't just color-related.

The latest edition of the *Maroon and White*, the school newspaper, came out on November 3. On the sports page, the sports editor, Roger Deromedi, wrote an article titled "The

Non-Monetary Value of Sports." The article was about the cost of running the sports programs at the high school. Deromedi pointed out that in 1969, City High had spent $18,000 on its sports programs and had turned a meager profit of $147. His point was that the money was better spent in such a way that supported more students. While his point made sense, it pissed off all the sports people. I thought it was a little odd that he was the sports editor of the school paper, when the closest he'd come to the field was as a part of the marching band.

The school paper wasn't the only news for the week. The midterm elections had just been held and the Democrats had swept Congress. Jimmy Carter was elected governor of Georgia and Ronald Reagan was reelected in California. Political news and events always swirled around us. It was even in my Spanish class.

Most of my classes were routine, with the exception of Spanish. The majority of the kids in high school didn't see the need in learning another language and considered it a waste of time. After all, English was spoken throughout the country. So unless you planned to live in Latin America, what was the point of learning Spanish, other than it was a requirement in order to graduate?

My Spanish teacher, Mr. White, was a little odd. He'd graduated from the University of Tennessee and was said to be fluent in Spanish and Chinese. At times, he appeared to be somewhat serious, but on other occasions, he came out with things that cracked us up. Some days he attempted to impress us with his Chinese-speaking skills. He rattled off what sounded like Chinese; of course, none of us knew what Chinese really sounded like, so we weren't sure whether he was really speaking the language or just jabbering nonsense. Hell, the only Chinese we'd ever heard was from a cook on a TV show like "Bonanza."

Then there were the days when Mr. White did Richard Nixon impressions. He held out his arms with the two-finger peace sign. Then he looked sternly at the class while shaking his cheeks as he quoting some of Nixon's famous phrases. He even sounded somewhat like Nixon. This was quite entertaining, even if it had nothing to do with us trying to learn Spanish.

Mr. White had replaced Don Smith and everyone had liked Mr. Smith, so Spanish just wasn't the same as it had been with Don Juan. Even Don Smith's car, his Chevrolet Impala convertible, fit in with the cool-car trend at City High. It was also the era of the muscle car and there were a lot of them in the school parking lot. On any given day, one could see a Z-28 Camaro or a Shelby Mustang. Some of our buddies also had some great-looking cars: Eddie Francisco's 1968 maroon GTX convertible, Randy S. Gray's Camaro, Jon Exum's silver Corvette, and Foster Yates's 1970 green Chevrolet Chevelle SS, just to name a few. In the mornings, you could hear them a mile away as they rumbled into the parking lot.

Mike O'Neil had recently joined the muscle-car club. His dad had bought him a brand-new bright-red Dodge RT Challenger, as a reward for his good grades the previous semester. There was a catch: Mike had to pay for the gas and maintenance. Of course, sporty cars consumed lots of gas. O'Neil and Foster Yates were like most high-school students and didn't have much money. So in order to supplement their budgets, from time to time they'd siphon gas from other students' cars. Now at the time, gas cost between 26 and 32 cents a gallon. Even though you could fill half a tank with a few dollars, those same dollars would buy a big meal at the Krystal.

One of their reliable targets was a Lincoln Town Car that a couple brothers drove to school. The Lincoln was their dad's car and it had a big gas tank that held over 20 gallons. O'Neil figured out that on Mondays, the large car's tank was full; generally, dads filled up their cars over the weekend. So Monday was the extraction day. The brothers made it an easy target. They parked it in the top parking lot and always backed into the space. The gas tank was located in the back right side of the car, so it was out of view from the driveway.

The gas bandits had their system down. Each had a five-gallon gas can and a clear plastic tube, which was about six feet long. The operation was simple: unscrew the gas cap, stick one end of the tubing into the tank, and make sure the other end of the tube was below the level of the car's gas tank. Next, one of them sucked on the tube until he saw the gas in the tube. The trick was to move quickly enough, otherwise you got a mouthful of gas. They let the gas run until the five-gallon can was full. When one can was full, they filled the second can.

This deed was done in broad daylight during school hours. The best time for the extraction was during class; obviously, most of the teachers were in class and not patrolling the parking lot. But to be on the safe side, the boys stationed a girl as the watcher, who signaled them if someone came close. Apparently, the brothers never caught onto the scheme. They probably just assumed the big car got really bad gas mileage, if they looked at the gas gauge at all. But O'Neil and Foster saved some of their gas money.

The Tempo Tap Room was one of Eddie Steakley's favorite hangouts. He always went there on Fridays before our games to drink a couple of beers. He said it helped him relax and focus on the game. After the Thursday practice, Steakley had gone to the Tempo Tap Room to drink and play the pinball machine for money; if you won, the bartender paid you off. Sure, it was illegal, but so was selling beer to anyone under the age of 21.

Steakley had been there for about an hour when two

Central players he knew happened to walk in. Steakley started running his mouth about how bad we were going to beat them.

They popped back at him, saying, "No way! Ya'll haven't beaten us in thirty years. All we have to do is just show up and we'll win the game!"

The spirited but friendly debate went back and forth for a few more minutes. Then the Central boys called Steakley's hand and said: "Do you want to bet?"

Steakley said, "Sure, and I'll give you twenty-one points!"

They shook hands and the bet was on.

When Pat Petty told me about the bet the next day at practice, I told him, "Is Steakley nuts? The most points we've scored in a game all year is twenty and that was against Kirkman!"

The Friday practice was a full-out scrimmage on the upper field. Coach Davis wanted us to be used to playing hard on Fridays and the scrimmage was the best way to do that. We were finished by five.

Some of the school clubs had their annual house parties that weekend. There was always something to talk about after a house party. We'd hear all about them on Monday.

Chapter 55

The House Party

Since there wasn't a football game scheduled, this was the week the school designated for both the girls and boys clubs to hold their annual house parties.

A house party was like a retreat for a school club. The members went off for the weekend to a campground that had cabins at the lake or in the nearby mountains. There, they reviewed the values of the club and the goals for the year. Sometimes, an inspirational speaker addressed the group. The rest of the weekend was for fun and getting to know one another. Sometimes the clubs took the fun part to the extreme.

Two years ago at the Civitans' house party, several members had been caught drinking beer in their cabins. So the Civitans had been banned from having house parties for the next three years. Last year, however, the Civitans had their own unsanctioned house party at Ray Gorrell's house. This year, of course, Ray was away at Columbia Military Academy with Arch Trimble. Arch's lake lot would have been the next best option, so it was determined that there would be no unsanctioned Civitan house party this year.

Several of the other clubs were holding their parties that weekend. The Hi-Ys were having their party at Lake Ocoee, about 20 miles east of Chattanooga.

After football practices, David Soloff gave three sophomore players from Signal Mountain a ride home. Soloff was one of my few friends in high school who smoked pot. It wasn't uncommon for him to light up as he drove around and he naturally offered the underclassmen a hit off his joint. They'd never smoked pot before, but they gave it a try.

Two of the three sophomores were pledges to Hi-Y and were planning to go to the house party at Lake Ocoee right after practice with some other guys. They thought it would be cool to take some pot to the house party, so they asked Soloff if he could get them some. Soloff had connections and had an extra bag of pot, so he gave it to them for the weekend outing.

Soloff was also a Hi-Y and was going to the house party, but not until late Friday night. The two 10th graders hadn't been there long when they went out in the woods to smoke. They got to what they thought was a secluded area and fired up the joint when one of the senior Hi-Y members came strolling through the woods and caught them. They were escorted back to the lodge for questioning about the pot by Coach Phifer, one of the chaperones; he wanted to know where they got the pot. After about 30 minutes, one of the boys broke down and told the principal that Soloff had supplied them with it. The boys were confined to the cabin for the rest the night and would be sent home the next day.

The coach and the senior leaders knew Soloff was coming up to the camp later, so they planned to search him upon arrival. One of the busted boys managed to sneak out of the bunk house and run down to the entrance of the camp, so he could warn David that a trap was waiting for him.

On the ride up to the camp, Soloff drank a couple of beers and smoked a joint, so he was feeling no pain as he turned off the main road toward the camp. The 10th grader waved him to a stop and told him what lay ahead. Soloff had three bags of pot and three or four beers with him. So he took them out of the car and hid them on the side of the gravel driveway under some leaves at the base of a large an oak tree, figuring he'd pick them up on his return trip home. Then he drove up the half-mile driveway to the camp lodge.

As he pulled up in front of the main cabin, Denny Cornett and Mark Eaton walked out to the lodge to greet him. David stopped the car and got out and asked them what they wanted. They told him they were going to search his car, because they believed he had pot. As they approached his car, Soloff, who was fueled with the beer and pot, got out, picked up a stick, swung it wildly in the air, and yelled: "You ain't going to touch my car!"

Cornett and Eaton backed up.

Coach Phifer came out of the cabin and wanted to know what was going on. Soloff put down the stick and regained his composure as he responded to the coach. He told Phifer that they wanted to search his car for no apparent reason and he wouldn't let them.

The Coach said, "We had some marijuana issues earlier tonight and we're checking everyone. We just need to check your car and bags to ease everyone's concerns."

David told Phifer that it was okay for him to check the car and assured him there was no pot. As expected, the coach didn't find any contraband. Then he asked Soloff if he'd supplied the two sophomores with pot and Soloff denied being the source.

The next day, the two pot smokers were sent home early, but Soloff stayed until the event was completed Sunday afternoon. He packed up his car and headed home, but stopped at the edge of driveway at the camp entrance to retrieve his pot and beer. He found the beer, but not the pot. He assumed a raccoon had found his stash. He guessed there was a happy raccoon somewhere in the woods.

After church that same day, my dad and I picked up Rick Spencer and headed to the gun club for a little target practice. Rick love shooting guns. He really appreciated that my dad took him out, since Rick's dad had died when he was a young boy. We spent the afternoon shooting skeet with shotguns, then shooting long-range targets with a variety of rifles. Rick was a fairly good shot, even if he didn't have much experience. It was a good way for me to take my mind off the big game, which was all I'd thought about since we beat Howard.

In five days, we'd see if we could break the 30-year hex.

Chapter 56

The Central Game

The Monday before the big game, the Civitans brought an old junk car to the east parking lot just outside the gym. The glass and engine had been removed, so it was just the body and four bald tires. The boys painted it purple and wrote in gold spray paint, "Pound the Pounders!" For the price of a quarter, you got two swings with a sledge hammer at the old car.

Normally, these types of spirit-building events were held during Homecoming week, but the Central match-up was the biggest game of the year, so it got all the attention and this fund-raiser was a big hit that went on all week. By that time, it barely resembled a car.

The City-Central game was a rivalry that dated back to 1905. The last time City beat Central was in 1939; City won the game 7-to-6. The two teams hadn't played every year since then, but Central had won all 19 of the contests played during this time period. Central was coming to this year's match-up with a record of 1 win, 7 losses, and one tie. They'd lost their last two games to East Ridge and Soddy Daisy; it was the Purple Pounders's worst season in two decades. Although Central was a different school now that it had moved to a new location and lost its legendary coach, it was still the game of the year for fans of both schools.

We'd now moved up to 14th in the state and were number three within our region. It looked as though the Dynamos might beat Central for the first time in over 30 long years and this was the game that the City High alumni and students were looking forward to with great expectation.

The sportswriters picked us to win the game, so the pressure continued to mount. Throughout the week, both papers ran daily articles about the historical clashes and the predictions for Friday night. The game was so popular that in years past, it had been played at UTC's Chamberlin Field. But this year's game would be played at Brainerd High School.

By week's end, we were tired of the hype and ready to play. Our two weeks off had been good, giving us time to get over some of those nagging injuries. Eddie Roberson had rested his sore ankle and he was at about 90% and ready to go.

Friday finally arrived; fittingly it was Friday the 13th of November.

We hoped this wasn't a bad omen for the boys in maroon.

Classes were held as usual, but most of the football players just hung out in the Commons or the Amory. There was no way we could focus on school work.

After lunch, we had the pep rally of the decade.

Colonel Creed Bates, known as Mr. City High, was there to address the entire student body before the big game—as he'd done almost every year since 1927. Colonel Bates had actually graduated from Central High. Shortly after graduating from Central, the United States entered World War I. He joined the Army and attended Officers Training School in Fort Oglethorpe, Georgia. He graduated as a Second Lieutenant in Field Artillery. Since Lt. Bates spoke French fluently, he was shipped off to France. After he was discharged in Germany at the closing of the war, Lt. Bates remained in Europe and studied in Paris. He later received degrees from Columbia, Stanford, the University of Wisconsin, Peabody College, and the University of Cuba. He returned to Chattanooga to teach at City High School for a couple of years, then moved on to be a principal. After a short stint as the principal at the newly opened Lookout Junior High

School, he became the principal of Chattanooga High School in the fall of 1927.

The Colonel served continuously in this capacity, except when he was recalled to service in World War II. He was attached to Special Services in England, where he taught mathematics to the troops and served as an interpreter. For outstanding service, he was awarded the Legion of Merit and was discharged as a Lieutenant Colonel. At the war's end, he returned to Chattanooga High and resumed his position as principal of what he called the "oldest and best secondary school in the South." He remained principal until 1964, when the school-system's mandatory retirement forced him to leave the job.

Although Colonel Creed had graduated from Central, his heart was at City. Probably no man understood the rivalry between the schools better than he did. Since his retirement, he'd come back to the pep rally before every Central game. This year was no exception.

As the rally began, the old Colonel sat on the stage with the other leaders. He was tall, white-haired, and fairly fit for his age. He wore a brown suit, white dress shirt, and maroon tie. When it was time, he got out of his chair and walked to the microphone. As always, he received a standing ovation. He waited for the clapping and hollering to calm down, then began to speak. You expected a big booming voice from the stately figure, but instead, his high squeaky voice reminded one more of a cartoon character. He always started out by saying how City was the oldest and the best, then continued to talk about the importance of the game. "Tonight, it's City's turn to win. I promise you that if we win, I'll be here Monday morning to lead the student body in the Snake Dance!"

I had no idea what a Snake Dance was until someone explained it was like a conga line that signaled a celebration. This—the old Colonel dancing through the halls of the school—I had to see. All we had to do was to win the game.

That afternoon we went through our normal dressing routine and boarded the bus for the 30-minute ride to Brainerd High. To our surprise, a large banner was taped to the ceiling of the bus. "Rip 'em Up, Tear 'em Up, Give 'em Hell, Pounders!"

Seeing it, Pat Petty said, "What the hell is this shit!" He reached up and ripped down the banner.

Then we noticed "Go Pounders," "Beat City," "Yea Purple," and "Dump the Dynamos" written on the windows in what looked to be lipstick. Come to find out our bus driver also drove the school bus for Central, so a group of creative Pounders decorated the bus. It pissed us off, but it was a clever trick.

With the sign on the floor, we drove out of the parking lot and not a word was spoken. As we pulled into the Brainerd parking lot, we could see that a good size crowd was already there. E. Blaine had driven to Cleveland and picked up my 80-year-old grandmother, so she could attend the game. Irene would join them, so I had a small family cheering section. My sister couldn't attend, but she sent me a Western Union telegram: "Lots of Luck to Broadway Buck, Love Sis."

Later, the newspapers estimated the attendance at 8,000, but most people thought it was closer to 10,000. Many believed it was the largest crowd ever to see a game at Brainerd High. The game was broadcast over the local radio. By 7:45, 15 minutes before kickoff, there wasn't an empty seat in the stadium. It was standing room only and that was at the west end zone.

We were once again wearing our all-maroon uniforms. Central wore white jerseys trimmed in purple, gold pants trimmed in purple, and gold helmets with a purple hammer on the side symbolizing the "Pounding."

We finished our warm ups, headed to the locker room, and

sat around the edge of the room. Coach Davis walked to the center of a solemn focused team. "Boys, you saw the size of that crowd out there. Well, most of them came here for one reason and that's to see us beat Central. You can make history tonight. But you have to stay focused and execute what we've practiced on all year. You've come a long way this year and there have been ups and downs, but tonight can be your night. Remember, we're a team and we play as a team."

Then he told us to bow our heads for the prayer. After we said amen, he said, "Are you guys ready to play some football?"

We all yelled, "Yes, sir!"

He concluded by saying, "Then let's go make history and kick their butts!"

We all started yelling as we ran out of the locker room, but as we ran onto the field, the cheering of the crowd was deafening.

Dr. Jim Henry, now the school superintendent who had played in this game in the forties, stood on the sidelines. He was joined by several old Dynamos from the past, including Bob Corker, who'd played in the previous year's game.

Central won the toss and elected to receive the ball.

The ball was kicked and the game of the year, or the past three decades, was underway.

In the first 10 minutes, neither team moved the ball with any consistency. We had held the Pounders and it was fourth and seven. On the last play of the quarter, Central lined up to punt the ball from their 44-yard line. It was a booming kick that was heading my way. I called for it and went back to field the punt.

As I got ready to catch the ball, I looked up and noticed a gaping hole on the left side. I could already visualize crossing the goal line and the headlines in the paper the next day reading,

"Broadway Buck Leads Dynamos to Victory!"

Unfortunately, I'd taken my eye off the ball. As it came to me, it slipped through my hands and hit the ground. In a panic, I tried to pick it up, but as I reached for the ball, it bounced back toward me and I accidentally kicked it—back about 10 yards closer to our goal line! I chased after the ball, but two Central defenders knocked me out of the way and they recovered the ball on our 11-yard line.

While the Central fans when nuts, I just laid on the ground wishing I could dig a hole and crawl in it. The biggest game in three decades and I fumbled a punt that would have surely led to a score and might even cost us the game. In the previous nine games, I'd fielded numerous punts and kickoffs, plus I'd carried the ball from scrimmage over 30 times, and I'd never, not once, fumbled the ball. Of all games to have my first fumble of the year, why *this* one? Now I visualized the next day's headlines to read: "Buchanan's Fumble Leads to Another City Loss to Central!"

The quarter came to an end and we switched sides on the field. The walk to the other end of the field seemed like the longest of my life. I looked straight ahead and didn't dare look toward our stands. I knew what they were thinking or saying to each other. "Hey, there goes number twenty; he's the one who dropped that punt!"

On the first play of the second quarter, the Pounders lined up on the 11, snapped the ball, and Jim Hunt ran to the six. On the next play, quarterback Randy Harris scored the game's first touchdown.

The Central fans went wild. If they beat us, it would make their season. The extra point failed, but with 11:36 left in the second quarter, the Purple Pounders were up 6-to-0.

I felt the weight of the entire school on my shoulders. I'd

fumbled a punt that led to a score. I was determined not to let my mistake cost us the game. I would play as hard as I could to see to it that we won the game.

Roberson returned the kickoff to the 35. We methodically moved the ball down the field and got on the scoreboard with a 20-yard pass from Wilder to Steakley. The extra point was good. The first half came to end and we led 7-to-6.

As we walked toward the locker room, I got another threat from Pat Petty about kicking my ass. At least this time, I deserved it. But what I was dreading was what Coach Davis had to say to me during halftime.

As we entered the locker room, I took a seat and the water boy handed me a cup. As expected, Coach Davis came over to me with a cup of water in one hand and a bottle of his heart medicine in the other. In a rapid-fire rant, he started my ass-chewing. "How could you take your eye off the ball! Not only did you make one mistake by dropping the ball, you made another mistake by trying to pick it up and kicking toward our goal line! Hell, you know better than that. How many times have we told you if you fumble a ball, just fall on it? Don't try to pick it up and run with it!"

He continued in that vein for a few more minutes. As he concluded the outburst, he took a big slug of his heart medicine.

I said nothing out loud, but I said to myself, "If it's not bad enough that my miscue might cost us the game, could it cause Davis to have another heart attack?" Now I could see a third headline in tomorrow's paper. "Buchanan's Blunder Costs City the Game and Their Coach!"

It was a long halftime and I was glad to be back on the field, where at least I had a chance to redeem myself.

Chapter 57

The Second Half

In the first half, our defense had played well and except for the short touchdown run after my fumble, Central couldn't move the ball on us. Our offense had moved the ball fairly well, but we'd only managed the one score. As the third quarter started, we hoped that would change.

We took the opening kickoff and began to move the ball down the field, all the way to the Central seven. We tried two running plays, but lost yardage on both of them. Then we got a short gain on another running play and it was fourth down. Rather than try for the field goal, Coach Davis opted for another play. Wilder rolled out to his right and hit Eddie Steakley with a short pass on the right side just over the goal line. Ronnie Stinnett kicked the extra point. Hey, we'd scored two touchdowns passing the ball. Maybe it was our night.

City led 14-to-6 with six minutes to go in the third quarter.

At the start of the final quarter on fourth and long, Central had the ball deep in their own territory. The punter was standing in his end zone. He shanked the ball, a really bad kick that we recovered at their 15-yard line. So we had great field position deep.

On the next play, right halfback David Sanders took a pitch from Wilder, swept around the left end, and sprinted into the end zone for the third touchdown of the night. Once again the extra-point kick was good. It really *was* our night: We'd kicked three extra points so far. Hell, we'd gone two or three *games* without kicking three extra points. Now the Dynamos were up 21-to-6.

As the ball was being set up for the kickoff, the Troop started another "off-standard" cheer: "Watermelon, watermelon, sitting on the vine, look on the scoreboard and see who's behind!"

I was feeling a lot better about our chances now and it looked like my muffed punt might just be forgotten.

With time running out for the Purple guys, Central took to the air. Harris completed a couple passes, then tried to throw deep. Fortunately, Gary Rundle, our sophomore safety, was in the right place. He intercepted the ball and returned it to the Central 42.

From that point on, we just ran right at them. The tired Purple defenders had little success stopping our running attack. Fullback James Lawson and Sanders did most of the work, bringing the ball down to the one-yard line. On the next play, Wilder called his own number and scored on a one-yard quarterback sneak. It had to be our night when the extra point was good. We were four for four! And we led 28-to-6.

After our score, Central continued to try to pass the ball. But Denny Cornett put an end to their last effort to mount a comeback by intercepting a Harris pass on the 48. From that point on, we held on as the clock continued to run.

I looked back on the second half, when our offensive line of Lee Abelson, Tommy Richmond, Joe Burns, and Pat Petty took over and just wore the Purple guys out. It seemed like our pulling guards, Richmond and Petty, were wiping out the defenders on every play.

Our defense played tough in all four quarters. After my fumbled punt in the first quarter, we shut Central down. On the night, they rushed for only 15 yards, passed for only 30, and threw three interceptions.

Our offense ran and passed and gave us a season-high 28 points. Even I somewhat redeemed myself. I intercepted a pass, made several key tackles and a couple of good runs, and fielded two other punts without fumbling.

As the clocked ticked down under a minute, the Troop broke out in the chorus of the popular Steam song and the rest of the student section joined in singing: "Na-nana-na-nanananananana, hey hey-hey, goodbye! Hey hey-hey, goodbye! Na nanana, nananana, hey hey-hey, goodbye ..."

When the game clock got to 10 seconds, the entire home side chanted the count down until the final horn sounded.

The home crowd went wild! The cheering and yelling were deafening. History had been made in two ways: We won the game 28-to-6 and recorded the best record in the school's history at 7 wins, 2 losses, and 1 tie.

The whole team rushed toward Coach Davis and hoisted him on our shoulders. We carried him to the middle of the field where he dismounted and shook hands with a dejected Coach Joe Lee Dunn of Central, who at the age of 24 had had a tough first year as a high school head coach. When asked later by a reporter what he thought about City's performance, he said, "I think City is the best football team we've faced all season. You can't take anything away from them. They played great."

As Coach Davis returned to our sidelines, he was greeted with hugs and handshakes from principals who spanned the 30-year drought: Colonel Creed, Dr. Henry, and Coach Phifer.

As for us, after we met the Central players for the traditional "good-game" sportsmanship greeting, we headed to our sideline where most of the students in the stands had rushed onto the field to congratulate us in our moment of glory.

The Troop boys, led by Spook and Foster, were high-fiving all the players and patting them on the back. LeBron Crayton was hugging all of us that he could get to. Kathy Huffaker greeted Wilder with a kiss. Susan Massey came down from the cheerleader platform to hug Randy C.

I paused for a moment and looked up in the stands; there, still standing in front of their seats, were E. Blaine, Irene, and my grandmother. They were still clapping. They gave me a smile and I gave them a big wave. As I turned to head toward the celebration, Cindy jumped into my arms and gave me a big kiss. Let the celebration begin!

It took a Friday the 13th on a cool November night to overcome 30 years of disappointment. It was our first win in the heated rivalry in 31 years and we were going to enjoy it as long as we could!

We yelled and sang on the bus. As we crossed the Tennessee River on I-24, once again I gazed out the window, looked at the river below and said to myself, "I made it back to the field and was part of history!"

When we got back to the Armory, Coach Davis went to all the seniors on the team, telling them how proud he was of them and that we were winners. When he got to me, he told me that despite the fumbled punt, I'd played a hell of a good game. He said, "Fumbles are part of life. You're going to have them. It's how you deal with them that makes a difference." He went on to say that he was glad I was on the team and I'd been a big part of our success.

It was clear he was emotional after all he and we had been through. This was truly his team; he'd coached most of the players since he became the head coach at City High. He'd had a near-death experience with his heart attack during the East Ridge game. I'd broken my hand and severely bruised my knee. The team had accomplished the goals set out at the beginning of the year, despite the adversities we faced. We'd all been through so much that it made the celebration that much sweeter.

Finally, I was thankful that I wouldn't be a headline in the paper the next morning. And we were all looking forward to seeing the Snake Dance on Monday!

We showered and most of us headed up Signal Mountain for the post-game party. It was a large gathering. The group was so big, it was held in a cul-de-sac in front of three houses of City High students. There were food and drinks for all and the music blasted from stereo speakers set up in one of the carports. Of course, there was some alcohol, but it was confined to cars and consumed outside. Evidently, the Signal Mountain police had been notified about the celebration, because they never showed up. It was a fun time—and one of the few parties where Steakley didn't pick a fight.

After the party, Mike O'Neil and I ended up at Garrett Strang's Summertown cabin at about three in the morning. It was a nearby place to crash, so we wouldn't have to drive off the mountain after our night of celebration.

When we got there, a light snow was beginning to fall. I went inside. Garrett had just gotten there about 30 minutes earlier from a date. While we were getting ready to go to sleep, we noticed O'Neil wasn't in the cabin. I went outside to look for him. There he was, passed out on the ground, covered in a light blanket of fresh snow. Garrett and I carried him inside. He never woke up. We put him on a couch fully clothed. Somehow, around 8:30 in the morning, O'Neil got up and went to work at the ice company. Garrett and I didn't rise until almost lunch time.

The coverage of the game dominated the sports sections of Saturday papers. Most of it focused on this historical City win. But there were a few views from the Central fan base. One fan said, "Well, it's about time they won a game. Even a blind hog finds an acorn every now and then!" Blind or not, we didn't care. We *had* won the game.

There were more parties on Saturday and into Sunday.

On Monday morning, it was back to school, but this would be a special day, a day for which City High School had been waiting for 31 years and it was finally here. We'd been told to report to the gym at 9:30 and all classes and activities would be delayed until after the official celebration.

I got to school at about 8:15. We'd planned a little pre-Snake Dance party. Some of the football players and members of the Troop gathered in the parking lot out by the Armory.

Steakley drove up in his old Chevy, got out, and opened up the trunk. There sat a Styrofoam cooler full of beer. It was his treat. He'd used the money he won from his bet with the Central players to buy the beer. We'd actually covered the ridiculous spread of 21 points Steakley had bet on—by one point! So for the next hour, we stood in the parking lot drinking beer out of paper cups.

At 9:15 we headed to the gym. As we entered the arena, the entire student body was on hand yelling and screaming at a deafening level, still celebrating the Friday night victory over Central.

The football team sat in chairs under the west-end basket. We were all wearing our white game jerseys. The cheerleaders, led by Sheron Bunch, marched onto mid-court. After the three or four thundering rounds of cheers, the door opened and in walked Colonel Creed Bates, grinning from ear to ear. He was followed by Principal Phifer, Superintendent Henry, and Coach Davis. The Colonel walked up to the microphone and before he said a word, he got a standing ovation accompanied by a roar from the students that was so loud that it could probably be heard in downtown Chattanooga.

Just before the long-time principal spoke, I looked over at the bleachers where the teachers were sitting and to my surprise, even Miss "Anti Sports" Prior was clapping and smiling. Hell, I didn't know the old lady *could* smile!

Colonel Bates began to speak into the mic and in his high-pitched voice proclaimed, "After thirty years of famine in the wilderness, it's wonderful to sit at the table of twenty-eight courses!" Then, mixing his metaphors slightly, he continued, "It has been a long lane with no turns. But we made that turn now and we will stay on it!" The old colonel stepped away from the microphone and the student body yelled, "We want Doc! We want Doc!"

Dr. Henry, who had graduated from City High school and had been a star football player himself, stepped to the microphone. His career in education took him from teacher to coach to principal and finally to superintendent. He said, "You have to have been a student, a coach, a dean, an assistant principal, and a principal for this to mean so much. I mean to your heart." He went on to say, "We had an important meeting at the Central office this morning, but there was the only one place I wanted to be and that's right here at Chattanooga High School!"

Then Coach Davis stepped up to address the students, who gave him a standing ovation accompanied by more deafening cheers, yells, and whistles. He made brief comments about the key players on the team. He then thanked the three assistant coaches. He emphasized their work and dedication to the program during his illness. Then one by one, the starters were introduced and got to address the cheering group.

As the last player finished his last words, the band started playing our alma mater. They played one verse before everyone began to sing the song to the tune of "Stars and Stripes Forever."

"Now, forward, we go to the fight. While proud waves our banners above, For purity gleams from its white, And maroon stands for power and love. Now hope points us onward to life.

While proud voices blend in happy chorus: Conquerors we in each strife. For CHS, for CHS we'll be victorious." The words were repeated a second time, but a little faster and, believe it or not, even louder.

As the song ended, the student body began to yell, "Snake Dance! Snake Dance! Snake Dance!"

With that, Colonel Creed Bates took off his jacket and started the march around the gym. Dr. Henry fell in behind him, followed by the football team, then the cheerleaders, then the entire student body. The cheering crowd followed the old colonel out into the parking lot, around to the front of the building, into the Commons, down the hall, and back to the gym. It was quite a spectacle.

Only six points had kept us from an unbeaten season that year. We'd surpassed the previous year's record and had finished with the best record in school history. But most importantly, we'd beaten Chattanooga Central High School for the first time in 31 years.

And we'd done it all after losing our coach for six games. But as I've looked back on it over the years, I clearly see that even though we didn't have Coach Davis to call the right offensive play or develop the winning game plan, he'd prepared us to get along without him. He taught us that the more we worked together, the more we gelled as a group, the more our differences disappeared. We weren't white or black. We weren't Jews or gentiles. We weren't rich or poor. We were the Dynamo football players and we were winners.

Joe Burns, Pat Petty, and Eddie Roberson would go on to make the First All-City Team, while Bill Wilder and I made the Second All-City Team. East Ridge won their final game of the year and edged us out for a spot in the state playoffs. We were invited to play in a bowl game, the Athens JC Bowl, on Thanksgiving Day. We voted to go to the game, but the bowl game was later canceled, so our season and most of our football careers were over.

But what a way to go out!

Epilogue

After football season, it was time to enjoy the rest of high school and get ready for college.

I turned 18 in December and had 30 days to register with the Selective Service system. This meant that I'd be eligible for the next military draft. On January 1, 1971, the state of Tennessee lowered the drinking age from 21 to 18. This was in response to outcries that a boy at 18 could go to Vietnam and run the risk of getting killed, but it was illegal for him to drink a beer. This brought a whole new dimension to our high-school experience. For one, we could now wear our letter jackets in the Tempo Tap Room without getting scolded by the bartender!

The class of 1971 graduated in June and headed in different directions. Many of us went to work, others to college, and some off to war. But the bond that was made during those high-school years would last a lifetime. As I did the research for this book, I reconnected with many old teammates and classmates I hadn't seen or been in contact with or heard about in decades. As we talked, it was like we just picked up where left off so many years earlier. We shared a lot of fond memories and could clearly remember many of the events we lived through during those crazy high school days.

But all the football players on the 1970 Dynamos team I spoke to or corresponded with reflected the influence Coach Davis had on us. Most of us have carried his life's lessons with us to this day and have applied them throughout our careers and lives. Our differences are merely superficial. All we have to do is see beyond them to understand that, in the final analysis, people working together can accomplish a great deal even against what may seem to be overwhelming odds.

The Schools

We graduated and moved on with life, but Chattanooga High School would never be the same. As time marches on and society changes, schools change along with them. When school began in the fall of 1971, Chattanooga's desegregation policy got more aggressive. A form of forced busing was imposed as students and faculty transferred among schools in an effort to achieve a racial balance. This happened between City and Riverside. Riverside's winning basketball coach Dorsey Sims came over to City to teach and coach. Coach Duke left City, went to Baylor, and became the basketball coach there. Two years later, Coach Phifer left to become the principal at Notre Dame High School.

These changes marked the beginning of the end for City High as we knew it, as the number of students attending the school on Dallas Road dropped steadily. By the early 1980s, enrollment reached a low of less than 200 students. Through the '80s and early '90s, the district made several attempts at revitalizing the student body, using the concept of the phoenix rising from the ashes, and the school became known as Chattanooga High School—Phoenix. Then, around 1990, a "school within a school" was formed by creating a magnet program for music, theater, and dance. After a few years of being a zoned magnet, the student population increased some.

However, the school was no longer able to support a sports program. The last year City High fielded a football team was 1998. They went 1-and-9.

Around 1999, programs expanded to include the creative arts in addition to the performing arts. The school now houses around 550 students in grades 6-12. The official name is, and has been since the creative arts inception, Chattanooga High School—Center for Creative Arts.

The building looks much the same as it did when we graduated in 1971, but the traditions that were built under the leadership of Colonel Creed Bates (who died in 1975 at the age of 81) are long gone. The campus may still carry part of the name as Chattanooga High School, but it's just a shell of what it once was. Today, the maroon and white Dynamos are only a memory.

As far as the other schools mentioned in the book, Central High School continues to exist and still fields a competitive football team. The Pounders are alive and well. But even today, at a Friday night game, the old alumni still talk about the glory days of football under Red Etter and the rivalry between Central and City.

Brainerd High also still exists, but their teams are now called the Panthers.

The Coaches

The high school coaches played a big part in the lives of their football players.

Bob Davis continued to coach at City until he died of a sudden heart attack in 1984 at age 52. During his 15 years at the school, he won over 100 games, with a 70% winning percentage. He earned his place in the school's history as its winningest football coach. But he's best remembered for the coach that broke the Central spell.

Coach Bob Davis
Chattanooga High School—Football Record

Year	Wins	Loses	Ties
1968	5	5	
1969	7	3	
1970	7	2	1
1971	7	3	
1972	9	2	
1973	8	3	
1974	7	4	
1975	10	1	
1976	9	2	
1977	4	6	
1978	7	3	
1979	4	5	
1980	8	2	
1981	9	2	
1982	9	1	
1983	3	5	
Total	**113**	**49**	**1**

Joe Lee Dunn only coached at Central for the 1970 season. The next year, he went back to UTC as an assistant coach. He then moved on to New Mexico, South Carolina, Mississippi State, Ole Miss, plus a variety of other football coaching jobs. He was the head coach at New Mexico and Ole Miss for short stints. Over his coaching career, he was best known for his aggressive play as a defensive coordinator. He continues to be involved in coaching.

Coach Red Etter is Tennessee's winningest high school football coach of all time; according the *Chattanooga Times Free*, he won 342 games during his remarkable career. He coached at Chattanooga Central for 27 seasons before moving on to the Baylor School, where he coached for 14 more years. His Central teams won seven state championships, while his Baylor squad took the title in 1973. That Baylor team also had the distinction of being ranked number one in the nation by one of the rating services. In 1984, Coach Etter received the National Coach of the Year Award presented by the National High School Coaches Association. Red retired in 1984 at the age of 70, after 50 years of teaching and coaching. That same year he was honored with the governor's Outstanding Tennessean award. Coach Etter was also inducted into the Tennessee Sports Hall of Fame. He died in 2006 at the age of 93.

The People

Many people were involved in this story and here's what happened to a number of them after they left City High.

Lee Abelson: He earned a BA degree from Vanderbilt University and an MBA from University of Tennessee at Chattanooga, then went on to have a successful business career. He married Iris Long, a Chattanooga girl, and they have two children. Lee now lives on Signal Mountain and has been quite active in local politics and volunteer work. He has served on the Baylor School Board of Trustees. He has also been an active participant in the Signal Mountain Playhouse as an actor, set builder, and as a Foundation board member.

Sharon Cable: The girl's all-star basketball player played basketball and volleyball at UTC, then later became the head women's basketball coach at UTC, the University of Kentucky, and Mississippi State. She was also the head volleyball coach at UTC. During her basketball coaching career, she won over 600 games in NCAA play, most of them in the SEC.

Bob Corker: The football and baseball player in the class of 1970 graduated from the University of Tennessee, became a very successful businessman, and got involved in politics. He retired from the business world and held a few appointed political positions. He was elected mayor of Chattanooga; from this position, he went on to represent the state as a U.S. Senator.

LeBron Crayton: One of the school's black leaders and basketball stars lost the ultimate game to cancer. After his last high school game his senior year, a loss to Bradley County in the Sub State playoff, he complained of severe pain in his knee. A few days later after a visit to the doctor, he was diagnosed with cancer of the knee. Shortly afterwards, his left leg had to be amputated—it was only a month before he graduated from City. The night after his surgery when he could have visitors, his room was standing room only with white and black students, a rare sight at that time. LeBron would lose the battle with cancer a few years later.

Roger Deromedi: The sports editor of the *Maroon and White* who wrote the article analyzing the cost of City's sport program versus the return on the investment went on to bigger things. After graduating from Vanderbilt University and earning an MBA from Stanford, he rose through the ranks of Kraft Foods to become the president and chief executive officer. For his next career move, he became Chairman of Pinnacle Foods based in Parsippany, New Jersey, with annual net sales of $2.5 billion (2012).

Mike O'Neil: He graduated from the University of Tennessee. He and I worked together for about 20 years. Of all the players on the team, he and I stayed in closest contact. We still talk to each other on a fairly regular basis. Mike now lives in Marietta, Georgia.

Eddie Roberson: Of all the seniors on the 1970 Dynamo

football team, only Eddie played football in college. He received a scholarship to Carson Newman in Jefferson City, Tennessee, but he only played one year. He graduated from University of Tennessee with bachelor and master degrees. He married a Red Bank girl and they have two daughters. He received a Ph.D. in Public Administration from The Institute of Government at Tennessee State University in 1998. He got into politics and was elected twice to the Chattanooga School Board, worked for the Tennessee Public Service Commission (PSC), and was appointed Chief of Consumer Services Division of the PSC. In 2006 he was appointed by Governor Phil Bredesen to be the director of the Tennessee Regulatory Authority (TRA) and was reappointed in 2008. He served as the agency chairman in 2007-2009. Eddie lives in Hendersonville, Tennessee, and is now a consultant specializing in energy and telecommunications. He is a published author of a book titled *Chaplain of Death Row*. Eddie is active in his community and his church. He is currently serving on the State Missions Board for the Church of God.

Tommy Richmond: Tommy graduated from the University of Tennessee. Shortly after graduating from UT, he and Marc Williams were duck hunting on the banks of the Hiwassee River. As Tommy was climbing out of the duck blind to get a shot at a flock of ducks as they flew overhead, he lost his footing and slipped. This caused him to drop his shotgun, which discharged, the blast hitting him under the right arm. Almost immediately, Tommy went into shock.

Marc reacted quickly and rushed to a nearby farmhouse to get help. Luckily, the farmer was in the yard starting up his tractor. He yelled to his wife to call an ambulance, then followed Marc to the blind. They put Tommy on a trailer hooked to the tractor and transported him to the road where the ambulance waited. They loaded Tommy in the back of the ambulance,

Marc jumped in, and off they went to the hospital in Chattanooga some 40 miles away.

By the time they pulled up to the hospital, Tommy had lost a lot of blood. The medic in the ambulance took his pulse and pronounced him dead. But they wheeled him into the emergency room anyway and began to pump blood into him as they removed the buckshot from his armpit and sewed up the wound. Thanks to Marc's quick reaction, Tommy survived. He had to go through an extensive rehab program to regain about 80% of the use of his arm and hand and live a normal life. He now lives in Knoxville. He had an extensive career at TVA and is now a consultant. He's married and has a daughter.

Arch Trimble: Arch recovered from his spleen injury and graduated from Columbia Military Academy and UTC. After graduation, he served as a First Lieutenant in the United States Marine Corp Reserve as an infantry officer. After his service, he went into the family insurance business. He established himself as a successful executive and a leader in the Tennessee insurance community. He married Vanessa Edwards and they had two sons. Arch contributed to this book, but unfortunately, he passed away before I completed it.

Eddie Steakley: Steakley could be a book by himself. He was a gifted athlete, talented enough to play college basketball or football. But after high school, he continued living a troubled life. He dealt with drug and alcohol problems and had several run-ins with the law. He even spent some time in prison. In his mid-fifties, Steakley knocked on the door of Eddie Roberson's dad, Marshall. The elder Roberson opened the door. There stood a tall, thin, bearded man wearing tattered clothes. The Reverend Roberson had known Steakley since he was in grammar school, but Marshall didn't recognize him at first. Then Steakley introduced himself to the retired pastor and was invited in. The once-gifted athlete told the old preacher that he wanted to turn his life around. Steakley asked Marshall to help him get to know Christ and repent his sins. That afternoon, he pledged his life to Jesus Christ and was saved. For the next few years, Steakley lived a Christian life until he died in his late fifties. I never saw Eddie after we graduated.

Rick Spencer: My old friend from junior high school graduated from City and went to UTC for a couple years. After his sophomore year, he joined the Army and signed up to go to Vietnam. Before entering the Army, Rick was a clean-cut boy who didn't smoke or drink. In the service, he volunteered to be a door gunner on helicopter gunships. He survived wounds sustained during that time and after his tour of duty, he returned home to Chattanooga. I saw Rick shortly after he returned; due to the horrors of war, he was a changed man. The once-church-going kid was now smoking, drinking, and into heavy drugs. About a year later, Rick turned up missing. He was found a few weeks later dead in a shallow grave at the gun range where my dad had taken Rick during high school for target practice. It was a drug deal gone bad.

Marc Williams: Marc graduated from the University of Tennessee. Shortly after graduation, he saved Tommy Richmond's life in a hunting accident; he remains humble to this day about his heroics. Marc had a successful career as a financial advisor. He married Nancy Strange, to whom Cindy introduced him when we were in college. They have two sons.

High School Sweethearts Still Together

Like a lot of high schools, City had its share of students who dated in high school and later got married. Perhaps surprisingly, a number of City couples remain married to this day. Most of them continue to live in the Chattanooga area.

Ted Bennett & Rosie Raulston: Ted was a football player from the class of 1970 and Rosie Raulston was the secretary of our senior class who had a long career in nursing. They have three kids.

Marvin Day & Karen McNichols: Marvin was a linebacker who graduated in the class of 1972. Karen played basketball and graduated with us in 1971. Karen had a long career in education.

Ward Gossett & Becky Dillender: Becky the basketball player married the sports writer. She graduated from City in 1971; Ward had graduated from Brainerd a few years earlier. They have two children. Ward still writes for the local paper.

Randy S. Gray & Susan Massey: The linebacker and the cheerleader got married. Both graduated in the class of 1971. Randy studied communication at UTC and the University of Georgia. He went on work as a freelance screenwriter. Susan was a nurse. They had two children. Susan passed away in the winter of 2015.

Pat Petty & Sharon Hudson: Pat and Sharon were obviously the youngest of our class to get married. Yes, they're still together after all these years. Pat went to work right after graduating from City High. He built a successful career in construction. They have two sons.

David Soloff & Kim Fuge: David was in the class of 1972 and married Kim who graduated in 1971 from GPS. David spent the majority of his career in the family construction business. They have three children.

Kenny Smith & Sammye Smith: From their first date after the baseball game, Kenny and Sammye have remained together and Sammye didn't even have to change her name. Kenny graduated from UTC, went into the electrical installation business, and got involved in local politics. He served on the school board and made a couple of unsuccessful runs for county council. They have two boys.

Bill Wilder & Kathy Huffaker: After graduating from Middle Tennessee State University, Bill joined Kathy's dad in the insurance business. He served as the CEO of Huffaker & Trimble Agency until the business was acquired by BB&T Bank. He serves on the boards of the United Way, the Chamber of Commerce, Bible in the Schools, and the YMCA of Metropolitan Chattanooga. Bill has also served as an elder at Signal Mountain Presbyterian Church. Bill and Kathy got married after school and have three children.

Buck Buchanan & Cindy Frazier: We both graduated from UTC. After graduation, I moved to Atlanta to take a job with Greyhound Lines. Little did I know at the time, but the first time she saw me in the halls of City High, Cindy told her good friend Sammye Smith that she was going to marry me. It took a little while for her prediction to come true, but it did. We got married on October 22, 1977. Our first son, Matthew, was born two years later.

In 1980, I changed jobs and industries, leaving the transportation business to go into the world of construction products with a job at Sto Corp. I stayed there for 15 years, working my way up from a sales rep to a vice president.

In 1981, our second son, Michael, was born. Two years later our daughter, Elizabeth, who goes by the name Lizzie, was born. Cindy spent the next several years taking care of the kids and running them from one place to another. I became a coach and coached the kids in whatever sport they chose to play; I spent most of my coaching time on the baseball field.

In 1996, I left Sto to work for Parex USA, a similar construction-products business where I held several management positions. In 2005 I became a vice president, managing a $100 million business unit. In 2006, with the kids now out of the house, Cindy and I left the South and moved to California. Who would have thought in 1970 that Cindy and I would be married nearly five decades later and living on the West Coast?

Over the years, I was very active in industry associations, served on several boards of directors, and became an industry spokesman. On the social side, I served as a deacon and elder in the Presbyterian Church.

Cindy and I have lived blessed lives. We have three great kids and three grandkids. We've had the opportunity to travel through our great country and abroad. I've had a successful and enjoyable business career. I continue to work at Parex and now hold the title of senior vice president. Today, we live in Yorba Linda, California. However, all of our children are now married and live in the Atlanta area. While we enjoy living in California, some day we will return to the South to be near our family.

It's been 45 years since that Friday the 13th night in November when the Dynamos finally beat the Purple Pounders. But it's a time that I will never forget.

Contributors

The following people contributed to the writing of this book. I thank them for their input.

Lee Abelson
Gretchen Archer
Cindy Frazier Buchanan
Allen Casey
Denny Cornett
Marvin Day
Karen McNichols Day
Priscilla Mitts Dietterich
Eddie Francisco
Bill Frazier
Mike Gist
Ward Gossett
David Jenkins
Gigi Galbraith LaPore
Steve "Spook" McKelvy
Mike O'Neil
Mike Pendergrass
Pat Petty
Tommy Richmond
Eddie Roberson
Garett Strang
Jerry Summers
Kenny Smith
Marvin Smith
Sammye Smith
Arch Trimble
Fred White
Bill Wilder
Marc Williams

Sources:

The Chattanooga Times

The Chattanooga Free Press

The Maroon and White

Wikipedia

The Chattanooga High School Year Books, 1964, 1969, 1970, 1971

The Chattanooga High School Pivot

Blackstone.com